Arthur Charles Hervey

The Authenticity of the Gospel of St. Luke

its bearing upon the evidences of the truth of Christianity - delivered at Bath in the

autumn of 1890

Arthur Charles Hervey

The Authenticity of the Gospel of St. Luke
its bearing upon the evidences of the truth of Christianity - delivered at Bath in the autumn of 1890

ISBN/EAN: 9783337369590

Printed in Europe, USA, Canada, Australia, Japan

Cover: Foto ©Lupo / pixelio.de

More available books at **www.hansebooks.com**

THE
AUTHENTICITY
OF THE
GOSPEL OF ST. LUKE:

Its Bearing upon the Evidences of
the Truth of Christianity.

FIVE LECTURES

BY

THE BISHOP OF BATH AND WELLS.

Delivered at Bath in the Autumn of 1890.

[SECOND EDITION.]

PUBLISHED UNDER THE DIRECTION OF THE TRACT COMMITTEE.

LONDON:
SOCIETY FOR PROMOTING CHRISTIAN KNOWLEDGE,
NORTHUMBERLAND AVENUE, W.C.; 43, QUEEN VICTORIA STREET, E.C.
BRIGHTON: 135, NORTH STREET.
NEW YORK: E. & J. B. YOUNG & CO.
1892

TO THE MEMBERS

OF THE

BATH AND WELLS DIOCESAN SOCIETY

FOR PROMOTING HIGHER RELIGIOUS EDUCATION,

THESE LECTURES ARE INSCRIBED

BY THEIR FAITHFUL SERVANT AND PASTOR.

ADVERTISEMENT.

THIS course of Lectures was delivered, and is now published, with the view of bringing within reach of those who have not easy access to many books, both the results of learned research into the history of the Gospels, and also some of the evidences of the truth of Christianity. I have, therefore, freely availed myself of the labours of others, chiefly those that are found in the list of books appended to each Lecture.

The abbreviations A.V. and R.V. mean the Authorised and the Revised versions of Holy Scripture.

SYLLABUS OF LECTURES.

LECTURE I.

The truth of Christianity dependent upon the truth of the Gospels; hence the supreme importance of being quite sure that the Gospel record is true. Attempts of the "Tübingen school" to prove the late date of the Gospels, in order to get rid of the supernatural element in the history of Christ. Baur. Robert Elsmere. Dr. Davidson's Introduction to the New Testament. Authenticity and age of the Gospels to be proved by external and internal evidence, and the concurrence of the two. Collapse of the arguments of the "Tübingen school." Bishop Lightfoot's Essays on Supernatural Religion. Special evidence of authenticity and age of St. Luke's Gospel derived from the "Acts of the Apostles." Previous necessity of proving the authenticity of "the Acts." External evidence of authenticity of "Acts of the Apostles." Testimony of Eusebius; the Muratorian Fragment; the ancient Syriac and Latin versions; Tertullian; Clement of Alexandria; Irenæus; Justin Martyr; Papias; Ignatius; Polycarp; and Clement of Rome. Internal evidence reserved for next Lecture.

LECTURE II.

Method of the advocates of the late composition of the Gospels and Acts for getting over the force of the external evidence. Historical accuracy of the Acts of the Apostles tested by its notices of historical personages, events, and places. Examples of this accuracy in the proper titles of different Roman governors; in the mention of Sergius Paulus, and the island of Cyprus; in the account of Ephesus, and the Diana of the Ephesians; in the name of the Magistrates of Thessalonica; account of Theudas. The Horæ Paulinæ. Omission in the Acts of Paul's visit to Damascus. Voyage and shipwreck of St. Paul.

LECTURE III.

Recapitulation of first and second Lectures. Object of present Lecture. Proofs that the writer of the "Acts" was present at many of the scenes which he describes. Proofs that the writer accompanied St. Paul to Rome. Proofs who could *not* have written the "Acts." Evidence in favour of St. Luke being the author. Luke's presence at Rome. Affectionate mention of him by St. Paul, proving that he was no new acquaintance. Agreement of St. Luke's style with the cultivation of a Physician. Time of the publication of St. Luke's Gospel deduced from the "Acts of the Apostles." Part II. Identity of authorship of the "Acts" and the third Gospel generally admitted as an undoubted fact. Examples of the same historical spirit and method in both, as regards chronological exactness, and use of the same words and phrases, medical and others. Evidence of identity from comparison of the close of the Gospel with beginning of the "Acts," from the same style of quotation running through both works. Another indication in the prominent place given to Peter in "Acts," as if to magnify the penitence of him whose denial of Christ he had recorded in the Gospel. Conclusion.

LECTURE IV.

Proof of authenticity of St. Luke's Gospel, irrespective of the "Acts of the Apostles." St. Luke's account of his own work. First generation of Christians dependent upon oral teaching. Immense importance to Church of having written authoritative Gospels. Three sources of Luke's information. External evidence of authenticity of Luke's Gospel. Eusebius. Muratorian Fragment. Irenæus. Justin Martyr. Marcion. Clement of Rome. St. Paul. Internal evidence. (1) Historical accuracy (a) as regards persons; as regards Herod and Augustus Cæsar; as regards Quirinius and the taxation; as regards Tiberius and the contemporary tetrarchs; as regards Pontius Pilate, and the relations of those petty rulers to the Roman government; as regards Annas and Caiaphas. (b) As regards minor incidents and allusions; payment of tribute to Cæsar; the parable of the nobleman going to a far country to receive a kingdom; the trilingual title on the Cross. (2) Agreement with other synoptic Gospels, and with St. John. (3) Fitness to be accepted as a true account of Jesus Christ. Conclusion.

LECTURE V.

Value and importance of evidence in all the affairs of life. Difference between trustworthy and untrustworthy evidence. Sufficiency of trustworthy evidence claims our belief as its right. Value of St. Luke's evidence tested. (1) As regards his personal character. (2) As regards his intellectual qualifications. (3) As regards his opportunities of acquiring exact and perfect knowledge of the facts and doctrines of Christianity: These last consisting of many years intimate friendship with St. Paul and his staff of missionaries; converse with divers apostles and evangelists and others; acquaintance with the holy places at Jerusalem, and access to various documents now lost. (4) By its being given before persons who had personal knowledge of the men and events to which his evidence related. The one qualification which St. Luke did not possess, that of an eye-witness. Comprehension by St. Luke's Gospel of all the cardinal doctrines of Christianity. Conclusion that belief in the Christian faith is the necessary act of a rational mind, and the duty of a moral agent, before whom the evidence is laid. Inspiration of the writers of the New Testament. Its nature and results. Comfort to the Christian reader of knowing that the writers of the Gospels were specially taught by the Holy Ghost. Conclusion.

THE AUTHENTICITY OF THE GOSPEL OF ST. LUKE.

LECTURE I.

THE Gospels—*i.e.* "The history of Christ [1]," as contained in the four Gospels—are the record on which the truth of Christianity rests. The Gospels tell us of the birth, life, teaching, miracles, death upon the cross, resurrection from the dead, ascension into Heaven of our Lord Jesus Christ, as historical facts in the past, and foretell His future coming to judge the world in righteousness. Those who believe this record to be true are called Christians. And the system of religion which results from acceptance of the Gospel story is called Christianity. But if the history of Christ contained in the Gospels is false, if either no such person as Jesus Christ ever lived in the world, or if He did not speak the words or work the works recorded in the Gospels, then Christianity is false, and all our hopes founded upon our belief

---

[1] Gospel. "The narrative of God," *i.e.* "The life of Christ." Skeat's Dictionary.

in its absolute truth, fall crashing to the ground. We are left to face sin, sorrow, death, and eternity as best we may.

Hence you see the immense importance of our having firm ground to stand upon when we assert that the Gospel record is true.

My purpose in the following Lectures is to lay before you certain facts and reasonings which seem to me to lead irresistibly to the conclusion that the Gospel record *is true,* and that we may without the slightest misgiving rest the whole weight of our hopes for eternity upon that record, as hundreds of thousands of souls have done for the last eighteen centuries and a half.

But before I lay these facts and reasonings before you, I wish to point out to you the special circumstances of our own times, which make it important that every Christian should be acquainted with some of the main arguments by which the authenticity of the Gospels can be conclusively established.

These circumstances are the vigorous and persistent attacks which have been made during the last hundred years upon the authenticity and the antiquity of the Gospels. An enormous mass of learning and ingenuity has been expended, mainly by German scholars, in endeavouring to prove that the Gospels were not written or compiled by the persons whose names they bear—Matthew, Mark, Luke, and John—but are the production of unknown writers in the second century. The motives for this contention are not far to seek. In the view of the whole school of critics, above referred to, it is a fundamental principle that anything supernatural, any interposition of God in the affairs of men in the way of prophecy, or revelation, or miracle, is impossible and incredible. But the Gospels contain distinct statements of such interpositions. There are the miracles wrought by Jesus Christ in healing the sick, opening the eyes of the blind, feeding the multitude with a few loaves, calming the storm, and raising the dead. There are the prophecies of Christ, say especially of the siege and destruction of Jerusalem by the Romans, which took place some thirty-seven years after our Lord's death. Above all there is our Lord's own resurrection from the dead, and His converse with the Disciples during forty days before His ascension. These things are stated clearly and distinctly in the Gospels. All the old attempts to explain them away, to account for the miracles by natural causes, to impute credulity or imposture to the Apostles, and so on, had utterly failed and been driven out of the field of argument. It was felt that if the Gospels really were the work of contemporaries and eye-witnesses of the things which they reported, the work of men who had companied with the Lord Jesus all the time He went in and out among men, and who gave certain evidence of their sincerity by devoting their whole lives to the work of preaching the Gospel without any earthly reward, and by laying down their lives as martyrs in defence of the Christian truth, it was not possible to give any rational excuse for not believing them.

But if it could be shown that the Gospels were not written by eye-witnesses, or contemporaries of the events related in them, but that they were written more than a hundred years later by persons who assumed the names of Matthew, Mark, Luke and John, then the case would be wholly different. In the course of one hundred years there was plenty of time for a whole crop of myths to gather round the name of Jesus Christ—just as later they gathered round the name of King Arthur or the Emperor Charlemagne, or famous saints in the legendary history of the Church—credulous persons disposed to believe the marvellous would credit them and propagate them; and the people amongst whom they circulated, not being contemporaries of the events, but separated from them by an interval of a century, would have no means of judging whether the account were true or false, accurate or exaggerated. Once establish the fact that the Gospels were not written till some time in the second century, and you might accept them as legends and not as history—you might accept the *natural* outline, and reject all the *supernatural* filling up of the picture.

To prove the late date of the Gospels became the great object of the sceptical school in Germany.

The great leader in one particular enterprise of destructive criticism was a German of the name of Ferdinand Baur. He was a man of vast learning, of immense ingenuity, and generally of great ability. By dint of extraordinary labour, great skill in arranging his facts and arguments, and great fertility of resource and expedients, he won over to his view, for a time, a considerable consensus in Germany, and even in England. His followers in Germany were called " The Tübingen school " from the University of Tübingen in Germany, to which they mostly belonged.

In England the best known writer on the destructive side is the anonymous author of

"Supernatural Religion." This author fully shares the opinion which I ascribed above to the whole school of sceptical critics of the impossibility and incredibility of miracles. To borrow Bishop Lightfoot's description of his book, "The first part undertakes to prove that miracles are not only highly improbable, but antecedently incredible." And the authoress of "Robert Elsmere" in like manner, representing after her manner the same school of thought, makes her hero say on his death-bed (of course to give it more effect) "miracle is to our time what the law (*i.e.* law of Moses) was to the early Christians. We must make up our minds about it... and if we decide to throw it over, as Paul threw over the law, then we must fight as he did. We must come out of it. The ground must be cleared. Then may come the rebuilding (p. 603)[1]."

Starting then from this fundamental principle of unbelief, that miracle is impossible, you see how important it would be to the sceptical school to be able to prove that the Gospels are not the testimony of good and veracious men as to what they had seen with their own eyes,

---

[1] Dr. Davidson's Introduction to the Study of the New Testament, in the later editions, is written on the same lines.

and heard with their own ears, and handled with their own hands, but the idle tales of a century later gathering round the true story of Christ's life, and repeated from one to another, when all who were alive at the time when the things were said to have been done had been long dead and buried. And in like manner you will see how important it is to the Christian believer to be certified that in reading the Gospel he is reading the testimony of eye-witnesses and contemporaries of the events narrated, a testimony which was circulated amongst the generation who were alive while Christ and His Apostles were living and acting in the world.

Now the evidences of the authenticity of the Gospels are of two kinds, (1) the external evidences; (2) the internal evidences.

(1) By the external evidences, we mean the testimony borne by early Christian writers to the existence of the Gospels, and their use by Christians, in their days: and the importance of such evidence is manifest. Suppose that no mention was made of the Gospels by Church writers for 500 years after Christ. You would naturally say if the Gospels really existed during those 500 years Church writers must have mentioned them. If they were read in the Church assemblies, if they were the ground on which

belief in Jesus Christ rested, and the source of men's knowledge of the life and death of Jesus Christ, Christian writers must have quoted them again and again. Their not being mentioned for 500 years is a clear proof that they did not exist. Being separated by such a distance of time from the events which they narrate, they are clearly untrustworthy. Evidently then early external evidence of the existence of the Gospels, and their use in the churches, is very important. We have this evidence abundantly, as I shall show you by and by.

(2) By the internal evidences, we mean the proof which the Book itself contains in itself, that it was written at the time, and by the author, at which and by whom it professes to be written. Let us take an example where the internal evidence would prove a book *not* to be authentic. Suppose you had a book which pretended to be written in the reign of George III, and on examining it you found some expression which showed that the writer had travelled by the railroad, you would say at once, this book could not have been written in George III's reign, because railways were not invented then. Or suppose you found in it the phrase "I wired to him to come immediately"

—you would say electric telegraphs did not exist in George III's reign, and there was no such word in use as "to wire"; therefore this book could not be written when it pretends to be. But on the other hand if the whole language, and all the allusions to events and persons, agreed exactly with all that you knew from other sources of George III's times, especially if several circumstances, not commonly mentioned in the histories of the time, but accidentally corroborated by private letters, or some collateral authority, were evidently known to the writer, you would say, "the internal evidence of the authenticity of this book is irresistibly strong."

When the external and the internal evidence tell the same tale, and mutually strengthen each other, our reason, if not clouded and borne down by prejudice, must yield its assent. And here I may state that the theory of the Tübingen school with regard to the late date of the Gospels is now generally considered to have collapsed. The arguments of Baur and the other destructive critics have been silenced by a battery of superior power. Scholars of equal learning have brought such an array of facts and arguments to bear upon the subject, that the boast that the "late date of the Gospels is one of the received results of modern criticism" can no longer be made. More recent and juster criticism has, on the contrary, utterly refuted it. In particular, the work already referred to, called "Supernatural Religion," which, when it first appeared, was cried up to the skies as a model of scholarship, learning, and critical sagacity, received such a dressing and such searching exposure of its fallacies and mistakes, from the pen of the late Bishop Lightfoot, that I imagine it can never lift up its head again as an authority on the matters disputed between them.

Still, I have thought it might be a matter of interest to you, and not without its use, to bring before you a special argument to prove the authenticity of the Gospel of St. Luke. If St. Luke's Gospel can be proved to be authentic it carries with it the truth of the whole Gospel story—the birth, the life, the miracles, the teaching, the death, and resurrection of our Lord, and confirms the authority of the other synoptic Gospels. And there happen to be peculiar means of proving the authenticity of St. Luke's Gospel which cannot be found in the case of the other Gospels. It is the Gospel whose existence and authorship is distinctly spoken of in another book of the New Testament, of the time of whose publication we have a distinct record in the New Testament itself.

You will all remember that the "Acts of the Apostles" begins with these words: "The former treatise have I made, O Theophilus, of all that Jesus began both to do and teach, until the day in which He was taken up" (Acts i. 1, 2). And that the Gospel according to St. Luke commences with a preface, in which the writer says: "It seemed good to me, having had perfect understanding of all things from the very first, to write unto thee in order, most excellent Theophilus, that thou mightest know the certainty of those things wherein thou hast been instructed." Putting these two passages together we learn (1) that the author of the Acts of the Apostles was also the author of the Gospel of St. Luke; and (2) that the Gospel of St. Luke was written before the Acts of the Apostles. It was "the former treatise." If, then, we can discover who the writer of the Acts of the Apostles was, we shall know at once who wrote the Gospel; and if we can make out the time when "the Acts" were written, we shall know the time *before* which the Gospel must have been written. But one other thing is necessary to make our work secure. We must be quite sure that "the Acts of the Apostles" is an authentic work. Otherwise we should be misled by it to mistaken conclusions.

Hence our Lectures must take the following course :—

1. We must demonstrate the authenticity of "the Acts of the Apostles,"
    (a) From external evidence.
    (b) From internal evidence.

In examining the latter, we shall find out who the author is; and this will add immensely to the strength of our argument. This will form the subject of this and of our two next Lectures.

2. We must examine the external and internal evidence of the authenticity of the Gospel of St. Luke, and show its bearing on the general evidences of the truth of Christianity. This will occupy our two remaining Lectures.

We proceed now to examine the external evidence of the Book called "the Acts of the Apostles." And I think I cannot do better than lay before you, first, not the most ancient testimony, but the most careful and comprehensive. I mean that of Eusebius, Bishop of Cæsarea, who was born about the year 260 A.D., and lived to A.D. 340. He is described [1] as "beyond question the most learned man and the most famous living writer in the Church" at the time of the

[1] Dictionary of Christian Biography.

Council of Nice, A.D. 325. Among other works which are still extant he wrote his Ecclesiastical History, in which he has preserved numerous extracts from many earlier writers, whose works are now lost. In this history he gives an account of the Apostles, and apostolic men, and of divers martyrs, and writers, and famous bishops, and heresiarchs; of the succession of bishops in chief cities in different parts of the world, from the time of the Apostles to his own time, and, in short, of everything which he thought of interest in connection with the Christian Church. Throughout his history he continually quotes " the Acts of the Apostles." He calls it " Holy Scripture " (p. 30). He says that Barnabas is frequently mentioned in " the Acts of the Apostles "; he refers to the election of Matthias in the room of Judas, to the election of the seven Deacons, to the martyrdom of Stephen, to the dispersion of the Disciples in consequence of the persecution, to the persecution by Saul, to the preaching of Philip in Samaria, to Simon Magus, to the conversion of St. Paul, to the conversion of Cornelius the centurion, to the Church of Antioch, and the Disciples being there first called Christians. He tells us that " Luke" relates in " the Acts " (p. 36) the mission of Paul and Barnabas to Jerusalem, the killing of the Apostle St. James by Herod Agrippa, and Herod's death, and that, again, Luke in "the Acts," brings in Gamaliel as speaking of Theudas and his death. A little later he bids us compare the account of Josephus of the Egyptian who made a great insurrection in the time of Felix the Governor, with what is said in "the Acts of the Apostles": "Art not thou that Egyptian?" Later, after mentioning that St. Paul was sent by Festus as a prisoner to Rome, and remained two years a prisoner, he adds, "And here Luke, who has left us in writing an account of the Acts of the Apostles, ends his history." In another part of the Ecclesiastical History (p. 59), speaking of St. Paul's companions, he writes thus: "Luke, by birth an Antiochian, and by profession a physician, a constant companion of St. Paul, and intimate with the other Apostles, learnt from them the art of healing souls, of which he has left us an example in two inspired books. The one is the Gospel of Luke; the other is 'the Acts of the Apostles,' which he composed not from hearsay, but having learnt them by his own eyes." The last quotation which I will give you from Eusebius is of a somewhat different kind, but perhaps still more important than those which have gone before. After giving some account of the several Gospels and their authors, he begins a new chapter (p. 77) by saying: "I will now sum up the different books of the New Testament. I must place first the holy quaternion of the Gospels. Then follows the book of 'the Acts of the Apostles,' then the Epistles of St. Paul (14), the 1st Epistle of John, the 1st of Peter, and, if you will, the Apocalypse. These are the books of Scripture which are acknowledged and received of all." Those which are questioned, he adds, though accepted as genuine by many, are the Epistles of James and Jude, ii. Peter, and the ii. and iii. of John.

Now I have gone thus fully—I fear so much so as to weary you—into the testimony of Eusebius, because of its great importance. Eusebius, from his great learning, and from his acquaintance with numerous early Christian writings which have long perished, from his intimacy as a young man with the greatest Biblical scholars of the age—Dorotheus, Pamphilus, and others of the school of Alexandria—from the opportunities of intercourse with other Churches all over the world which his position as Bishop of Cæsarea, and his favour with the Emperor Constantine, gave him, represents not only his own private opinion, not merely the authority of the Churches of Palestine, but the consensus of the whole Christian Church of the East and West as to the Canonical books of the New Testament. And when you recollect that in those days there were no printed copies of the Scriptures, and no railway communication between Antioch and Rome, and Alexandria, and the Churches of Africa, you will see the utter impossibility of an agreement as to a Canon of Scripture, comprising upwards of 20 distinct books, existing throughout the whole Christian world, unless these books had been from the earliest days of Christianity known to be genuine and authentic works.

But to proceed with other external evidences.

About the year 1740 an Italian scholar, Muratori, found in the library of St. Ambrose, at Milan, a MS. which had been brought thither from the library of Bobbio—St. Columbine's famous monastery in Lombardy. This MS., very badly spelt, and mutilated at both ends— now commonly called "the Muratorian fragment"—begins abruptly with a portion of the Canon of the New Testament Scriptures. After three or four words, evidently relating to the second Gospel, the MS. proceeds: "The third Gospel, that according to Luke, was written by Luke the physician, who was taken by Paul as his companion. He begins his Gospel with the birth of John the Baptist." The MS. then gives a҈ account of the "fourth Gospel," and a quotation from the first Epistle of John, showing that John was an eye-witness of what he relates, and proceeds, " But th҉ Acts of all the Apostles are written in one Book, in which Luke recites to the most excellent Theophilus all the things which were done while he himself was present." And then follows an enumeration of the other Canonical Books: St. Paul's Epistles to Seven Churches (nine Epistles), one to Philemon, one to Titus, two to Timothy, in all thirteen (the Epistle to the Hebrews not being reckoned), the Epistle of Jude, and two Epistles of John, and the Apocalypse. The two Epistles of Peter, and that of James are omitted. But we may say generally that the list is the same as that of Eusebius.

Now we are able to fix the date of this fragment within a very few years, by the mention in it of the "Shepherd" by Hermas, as quite lately (*nuperrime*) written in the lifetime of the writer (*temporibus nostris*), and in the Episcopate of Pius, Bishop of Rome. This suggests A.D. 170 as the latest date when this fragment was written. That is to say, nearly 150 years before Eusebius we find a catalogue of the books of the

New Testament universally received in the Catholic Church, given by this unknown writer at Rome, nearly identical with that of Eusebius writing in Palestine, and among them "the Acts of the Apostles" expressly ascribed to Luke as the author.

You see how very strong this evidence is.

But it is followed up by another. The New Testament was in very early days translated from the original Greek into the language of the different Churches. The oldest of these versions is that called the Peshito, in the Syriac language. It is considered by the most competent scholars to have been made before the year A.D. 150. It contains all the books of our present Canon, except ii. and iii. of John, ii. Peter, Jude, and the Apocalypse (and nothing else), and consequently the Acts of the Apostles, with which we are now concerned, and shows that in the early part of the second century "the Acts of the Apostles" existed, and that the book was held to be a portion of the Holy Scripture.

Another very ancient version is the Old Latin. It is so ancient that there are no means of ascertaining its exact age, but it is probably as old as, if not older than, the Peshito. The books of the New Testament contained in it are the same as those in the Canon of the Muratorian fragment above quoted. Especially it contained the Acts of the Apostles. Thus we learn that in the African Churches, for whom this Latin Version was made, as well as in the Syrian Churches, the Acts of the Apostles were considered a part of the Holy Scripture certainly as early as the middle of the second century, probably much earlier.

A third class of evidence, besides that of the ancient Canons of Scripture, and that of the most ancient versions, consists of accidental quotations from " the Acts of the Apostles," or references to its contents to be found in early Christian writers. The early works which have come down to us, I mean works of the first and early part of the second centuries, are so few, and for the most part so comparatively short, and it is so completely a matter of accident whether the subject in hand led these writers to quote from any particular book of the New Testament, that we cannot be surprised if such quotations are rare. But they are abundantly sufficient for our purpose, which is to show that the book called "the Acts of the Apostles" existed in the first and second centuries, and was well known to Christians of that primitive age.

We will begin with Tertullian, a famous writer of the African Church, at the end of the second century and beginning of the third. His works fill three volumes, and are on a great variety of subjects. Some are addressed to the Heathen, some to Heretics, some to the Church. Now, if you put together all the passages scattered through his works in which reference is made to "the Acts of the Apostles," or events related in that book are spoken of, you have almost a continuous history, from the forty days during which our Lord abode with the Apostles before the Ascension down to St. Paul's being stung by a viper in the island of Malta. The Ascension, the choice of Matthias, the Pentecostal effusion of the Holy Spirit, St. Peter's sermons, the selling of their lands by the Christians, the death of Ananias, the martyrdom of Stephen, the persecutions and the conversion of Saul, the baptism of Cornelius by Peter, the Council of Jerusalem, St. Paul's preaching at Athens, the prophecy of Agabus concerning St. Paul's imprisonment, the tears and entreaties of the disciples who heard it, St. Paul's visit to the Temple, his trial before Felix and before Agrippa, with many other details, are all referred to by Tertullian in one work or another; and "the Acts of the Apostles," or otherwise "the commentaries of Luke," are repeatedly cited by name.

Clement, of Alexandria, was born about A.D. 150, and was a Presbyter in the Church of Alexandria, and Head of the Catechetical School there. A considerable number of his works have been preserved entire. In them he largely quotes the books of the New Testament, as well as the Old, and among them, as Lardner tells us, has borne frequent testimony to "the Acts of the Apostles," as written by Luke. To quote a single passage, in his book called "Stromata," he says, "Luke, in 'the Acts of the Apostles,' mentions St. Paul as saying, Ye men of Athens, I perceive that in all things you are too superstitious." (See too Westcott on the Canon, p. 343.)

Irenæus was a little earlier than Clement. He became Bishop of Lyons about the year A.D. 177, and so was born probably between the years A.D. 120 and A.D. 130, though some place him earlier. In his youth he had seen and heard Polycarp, Bishop of Smyrna, and the disciple of St. John, who was martyred A.D. 155 or 156 (Lightfoot, p. 264). His immediate predecessor in his Bishopric, Pothinus, was a very old man, whose early youth must have coincided with the last years of St. John's old age. Well! Irenæus everywhere speaks of the Scriptures exactly as we do now, and quotes and reasons from the Gospels, the Acts, the Epistles, exactly as we do in this nineteenth century. But to confine ourselves to "the Acts of the Apostles," which is the book we have to do with now. In the third book of his great work on Heresies, ch. xii., on "The Doctrine of the Apostles," he begins with Acts i., the election of Matthias in the room of Judas; goes on to Acts ii., the descent of the Holy Ghost; gives large quotations from St. Peter's speeches; follows word for word the early history in the Acts of the miracles and preaching of John and Peter; quotes Peter's discourse at the Baptism of Cornelius the Centurion; the preaching of Philip to the Ethiopian Eunuch; the preaching of St. Paul at Damascus, and at Athens; the preaching of Stephen; gives the speeches of Peter and James at the Council of Jerusalem; St. Paul's Address to the Elders at Miletus; and many other extracts from the book which he calls "the Acts of the Apostles," and describes as "Luke's testimony concerning the Apostles." (Ch. xiii. at the end.)

You will note the extreme value of so full a testimony from so learned a man, separated by only one life from the life-time of St. John.

Justin Martyr, who was born at the opening of the second century, never quotes the Scriptures either of the Old or New Testament, chapter and verse, but in all he writes to either

Jews or Gentiles shows himself thoroughly acquainted with them. Speaking of the Gospels, which he says were read in the Christian assemblies on the Lord's Day, he calls them memoirs of the Apostles. As regards the Acts there are three passages (quoted by Lardner), which are evidently derived from the vii, xiii, and xxvi chapters of the Acts.

Thus, Acts vii. 20, 22, we read " In which time Moses was born," and " Moses was learned in all the wisdom of the Egyptians." Justin Martyr, writing to the Greeks, says that " Moses was not only born among the Egyptians but was counted worthy to partake of all the learning of the Egyptians," where observe the verbal identity (ἐπαιδεύθη—παιδεύσεως) and the sequence of thought, "was born and was learned," and "was not only born but was counted worthy to partake of the learning, &c."! (Ad Græc. cohort. p. 11.)[1]

Acts xiii. 27. "But they that dwell at Jerusalem because they knew him not (ἀγνοήσαντες), nor yet the voices of the Prophets which are read every Sabbath day, they have fulfilled them in condemning Him." Justin Martyr says, "The Jews who had the prophecies, and always expected the coming of Christ, knew Him not, and not only so but killed Him." (ἠγνόησαν).

[1] Morell's edition.

Compare, too, what follows about the Gentiles with Acts xiii. 44–48. (Apolog. ii. p. 85.)

Acts xxvi. 22–23. "Saying none other things than those which the Prophets and Moses did say should come, that Christ should suffer (παθητὸς ὁ χριστὸς), and that He should be the first which should rise from the dead." Justin Martyr says, "It had been obscurely declared by the Prophets that Christ should suffer (παθητὸς γενησόμενος), and after that be Lord of all." (Dialog. p. 302.)

In all the above places identity of phrase, coupled with identity of thought, makes it certain that Justin Martyr was acquainted with the Acts of the Apostles.

And now, lastly, we come to those three or four writers who may be said to border upon Apostolic times, Papias, Ignatius, Polycarp and Clement of Rome. Their writings are very few; their subjects did not necessarily lead them to refer to the Acts of the Apostles at all, yet everyone does as a matter of fact refer to things, or use phrases, which show that they were acquainted with the Book. Papias, A.D. 116 (as quoted by Eusebius), refers to Barsabas, surnamed Justus (Acts i.), and to the daughters of Philip the Evangelist (Acts xxi.), Ignatius, A.D. 107 (Bishop of Antioch), referring to our Lord's eating and drinking with the Apostles after the resurrection, uses the identical words of St. Luke in Acts x. 41, having immediately before quoted from Luke xxiv. 39. Polycarp, A.D. 108 (to the Philippians), uses the identical words of St. Peter in Acts ii. 24, speaking of the resurrection of Christ, followed up by quotations from St. Paul's Epistles. Clement of Rome, A.D. 96, applies to the Corinthians the saying of our Lord recorded, Acts xx. 35, "It is more blessed to give than to receive," and, in quoting Psalm lxxxix, he quotes it not as it is in the Septuagint, but as St. Paul quotes it, Acts xiii. 22, making it all but certain that he read "the Acts" as well as the other books of the New Testament to which he refers.

And thus much must suffice for the external evidence of the authenticity of "the Acts of the Apostles," a book you will remember which is to be one of our chief witnesses for the authenticity of the Gospel of St. Luke. We have seen a continuous stream of witnesses from all parts of the world, from A.D. 300 to A.D. 96, all acquainted with the book called the Acts of the Apostles, ascribing it without the smallest doubt to St. Luke as its author, and treating is as Holy Scripture. I cannot imagine any one, having only this evidence to go by, having the smallest doubt as to the genuineness of the book. The evidence in itself is conclusive, absolutely conclusive. But, suppose when we come to examine the internal evidences we find them telling a different story. Suppose we find the Book when we look at it through the critical microscope, full of contradictions, anachronisms, historical blunders, evidences of a later age, stories unworthy of Apostles and inconsistent with known facts, what shall we say then? We shan't know what to believe. We shall be as puzzled as a jury is with the contradictory evidence of two Irish witnesses. But if on the contrary the closest scrutiny of the internal evidence only reveals truth, harmony, accurate knowledge of contemporary things and persons, the utmost simplicity of purpose, and the most straightforward pursuit of truth; if the characters pourtrayed are replete with the dignity of true holiness, and worthy of their vocation as the servants of Jesus Christ; then this coincidence of the internal with the external evidence will come home to us with irresistible power; it will come like a steam-hammer to rivet our conviction so fast and so sure, that it can never be moved; and all the taunts of profane scoffers, and all the questionings of fanciful critics, and all the scepticism of men of science, and all the blandishments of infidel novelists, will pass by us as idle winds.

and leave us in the possession of an established faith—leave us strong in the Lord and in the power of His might, to believe His Holy Word, to work His Holy will, and to wait in the full assurance of hope for the coming of His Heavenly Kingdom.

But this internal evidence must be for our next Lecture.

LIST OF BOOKS CHIEFLY USED IN THE FOREGOING LECTURE.

Bishop Lightfoot's Essays on Supernatural Religion.
Robert Elsmere.
Dictionary of Christian Biography.
Eusebius' Ecclesiastical History.
Tertullian's Works.
Works of Irenæus.
Justin Martyr's Works.
Lardner's Credibility of the Gospel History.
Westcott's Canon of Scripture.
Salmon's Introduction to the New Testament.

LECTURE II.

WE completed in our last Lecture the external evidence of the authenticity of "the Acts of the Apostles," and are to follow up the subject by considering the internal evidence of its authenticity: our object being to ascertain that we have in "the Acts" a thoroughly dependable witness for the age and authorship of the Gospel of St. Luke.

But before we proceed with the proper subject of to-night's Lecture, I wish to say a few words to meet an enquiry which I think must have arisen in the minds of my thoughtful hearers, viz. how do the advocates of the late composition and unknown authorship of the Acts of the Apostles get over the mass of external evidence in favour of its early composition, and in attestation of the authorship of St. Luke? I will tell you. We have seen that there are no voluminous Christian writers in the first half of the second century. The direct evidence of such writers as Tertullian, Clement of Alexandria, and Irenæus of Lyons, does not reach much earlier than the year A.D. 150. Therefore, it is thought that by fixing about the year A.D. 120 for the publication of the Gospels and Acts, there is a possibility that in the course of thirty years these books may have spread through the whole Christian world, may have deceived Christians of every nationality, and been accepted as the Canonical writings of Apostles and Evangelists by all the Churches of Europe, Asia, and Africa, without a single suspicion or protest being raised against them! And with regard to those briefer references to things mentioned in the Acts, and the repetition of sentiments or phrases found in them, by writers at the end of the first and the beginning of the second century, the answer is, "Oh! these things were not taken from the Gospels and Acts which we now have in our Bibles but from some Apocryphal book which has since perished, or they were learnt from oral traditions which were still floating among Christians in those early days. You can't prove that Justin Martyr, and Papias, and Ignatius, and Polycarp, and Clement of Rome took their quotations from the Gospels or the Acts, though they happen to use the same words." Such is, in substance, the way in which the external evidence is met by the opponents of the authenticity and genuineness of the Acts of the Apostles.

We will now proceed to consider in some detail the internal evidences—*i.e.* the proofs which the Book itself contains that it was written at the time, and by the person, viz. St. Luke—to which it is unanimously ascribed by the Church of the first few ages of Christianity.

We will take first its historical accuracy. And I will ask you to observe that a work which, like the Acts of the Apostles, deals from beginning to end incidentally with historical events and personages is liable to detection at every step if it is inaccurate. Consider the number of historical persons with whom the narrative in the Acts is connected. There are the High Priests, Annas and Caiaphas; there is Gamaliel the famous Rabbi, and Judas of Galilee the turbulent patriot; there is Candace, Queen of the Ethiopians; there is the Emperor Claudius; there is Herod Agrippa, the King of Judea; there is Sergius Paulus, the Pro-Consul of Cyprus; there is (involved in the narrative though not named) Aretas, the Arabian King of Damascus; there is Annæus Gallio, the Pro-Consul of Achaia; Felix and Festus, the Roman Governors or Procurators of Judea; King Agrippa and Bernice; Drusilla the Jewess, the wife of Felix; and the Emperor Nero. The least mistake in chronology, or in general statement, concerning any of these personages would be detected at once in the light of profane history. Then consider the number of historical circumstances involved : the relative position of the Sadducees and Pharisees at Jerusalem at this particular time; the political condition of the Jewish nation ; the relation of their Kings to the Roman Government ; the peculiar circumstances of the different towns, as Cæsarea, the principal sea-port of Syria and the headquarters of the Roman military government ; Philippi, a Roman colony ; Thessalonica, a free Greek city ; Athens and its Areopagite court ; Ephesus and the fanatical worship of Diana ; Alexandria and its traffic in corn with Italy ; Damascus and its streets ; Jerusalem with its temple services ; and Rome with its colony of Jews returned from their banishment by Claudius. How difficult for any one to be accurate in all these things, if writing sixty or seventy years afterwards, though comparatively easy if writing of things in the midst of which he is actually living, and which he knows by his own senses of seeing and hearing. A few examples will, I think, illustrate the truth of this.

You are aware that at the time when the

events in the Acts of the Apostles took place almost the whole known habitable world (ἡ οἰκουμένη) was under the government of the Romans. Their vast empire in Europe, Asia, and Africa, was divided into provinces, each with its governor, just as our different colonies are managed by governors, Governor-General of India, and so on. But the Roman provinces (at the time with which "Acts" is concerned) were of two kinds, those which were in the gift of the Senate, and those which were in the gift of the Emperor. The provinces in the gift of the Senate were called Consular Provinces, because the governors of these provinces had always previously served the office of Consul at Rome, and in their provinces were styled Pro-Consuls (ἀνθύπατοι) (as in the Revised Version of Acts xiii. 7, xviii. 12, where Pro-Consul is substituted for the Deputy[1] of the A.V.). The provinces in the gift of the Emperor were called Prætorian, because they were under a military governor, a Prætor, who in his province was variously styled either a Pro-Prætor (ἀντιστράτηγος) or, more commonly, as one sent by the Emperor and representing his power, a Legate (πρεσβευτής)[2]; or by

---

[1] The Viceroy or Lord-Lieutenant of Ireland used to be called the Deputy of Ireland.
[2] Essays on Supernatural Religion, p. 292, and articles

a more general military term (ἡγεμών) the Governor. Now, if the Consular Provinces had always r mained such, and the Prætorian Provinces had always continued in the patronage of the Emperor, there would have been no great difficulty in giving the governors their right names. But this was not the case. It frequently happened that if there was a disturbance in any province which required more strict military discipline, or if for any other reason the Emperor wished for any particular province, he would exchange provinces with the Senate, and thus, what had just before been a Consular province became a Prætorian province, and what had hitherto been a Prætorian province became a Consular one, and was consequently governed by a Pro-Consul. Take the case of Cyprus, mentioned Acts xiii. Dio Cassius tells us that, in the distribution of the provinces by Augustus Cæsar, Cyprus, along with Syria, Cilicia, Phœnicia, and Egypt, fell to the lot of the Emperor. They were consequently Prætorian provinces, and are so described by other authors. Hence the critics were sore puzzled when they read in Acts xiii. 7, 8, 12, that Luke called the Governor Pro-Consul, or Deputy. The adverse critics were

Province and Praetor, in Dictionary of Greek and Roman Antiquities.

delighted to catch St. Luke making a mistake, and the friendly critics were at their wits' end to find excuses and explanations for him. Curiously enough, they had all overlooked the passage in the same historian (Dio Cassius), in which he tells us that later in his reign Augustus gave back Cyprus and Galatia to the Senate, and took to himself Dalmatia in exchange. So St. Luke was right after all. Sergius Paulus was Pro-Consul (Deputy) of Cyprus. And to crown the testimony to St. Luke's accuracy there have been found in Cyprus Roman coins of that age; one of these had on it the well-known head of the Emperor Claudius, and the inscription: Ti. Claudius Cæsar, on one side, and on the other, the inscription: Of the Cyprians, *Cominius Proclus*, Pro-Consul. And an inscription found in the same island within the last twenty or thirty years, of about the same date, actually has the name of Paulus, Pro-Consul[1], doubtless our very Sergius Paulus.

Cyprus appears to have twice changed hands subsequently. Under the Emperor Adrian, *i.e.* about the year A.D. 120, when our critical friends place the composition of the Acts, it was an Emperor's province, governed by a Pro-Prætor;

---

[1] Essays on Supernatural Religion, p. 294. Comm. on Acts in Bishop Ellicott's Commentary.

and again, a few reigns later, it reverted to the Senate, and was governed by a Pro-Consul again.

In the other instance in which the author of "the Acts" designates the governor of a province as Deputy or Pro-Consul, I mean the case of Annæus Gallio, Deputy of Achaia, in Acts xviii., we have a still more striking instance of the accuracy of the writer. I cannot do better than read what Lewin says (Life of St. Paul, vol. i. p. 271). "In the time of Augustus, Achaia (of which Corinth was the capital) was allotted to the Senate, and governed by Pro-Consuls; but under Tiberius (his successor) it was transferred to the Emperor, and governed by Pro-Prætors. In the fourth year of Claudius (A.D. 44) it was restored to the Senate and again became Pro-Consular." This was only eight or nine years before St. Paul went to Corinth. It is perhaps worth adding that the very mention of Gallio as Pro-Consul is a strong indication of the writer of the Acts being a contemporary. There is no extant account in secular history either of Gallio's Consulship, or his Pro-Consulship. We should be without any secular confirmation of the statement in the Acts, that Gallio was Pro-Consul of Achaia when St. Paul went to Corinth, if it were not for two chance passages in classical writers. Pliny, the author of the Natural History, speaking of the benefit of a sea-voyage to persons in a consumption, adds, "As I remember was the case with Annæus Gallio after his Consulate." And his own brother Seneca, quoting an expression of his brother Gallio's that "the disease was in the place, not in himself," says that he spoke it "when he was beginning to have a fever in Achaia." It may be added that profane history shows that Gallio's government must have fallen between the years 49 and 63. St. Paul's visit to Corinth was about A.D. 52 and 53 [1].

The author of the Acts was equally correct when he spoke of Felix and of Festus as Governors, *i.e.* having the title of ἡγεμών (Acts xxiii.–xxvi.). They were the Emperor's officers, not the Senate's, and though they were Procurators, not Pro-Prætors, they were rightly styled Governors (ἡγεμόνες) as they had Prætorian powers[2]. See Josephus, A. J. xviii., iii., 1.

I hardly know whether it is worth adding that we have another example of the accuracy which I have been illustrating in the use of the proper titles of Roman Governors, in the case

[1] According to Lewin (Life of St. Paul, vol. i, p. 274. The Chronology in Bagster's Bible places it A.D. 54, 55.

[2] Dictionary of Greek and Roman Antiquities.

of Publius, who in the xxviiith chapter of the Acts is styled πρῶτος, A.V., "the chief man" of the island of Malta. It appears from two inscriptions, one in Greek and the other in Latin, that πρῶτος, or primus, first or chief, was the technical name of the Governor of Malta, which was a dependency of Sicily. The Greek inscription runs *Prudens a Roman knight chief* (πρῶτος) *of the Maltese*. Malta had belonged to the Carthaginians. It looks as if πρῶτος, or Primus, was a translation of Rosh or Resh, the Punic for head or chief, and that in Carthaginian times the Governor of the island had been so designated like the Resh-ha-Gelutha, the Prince of the Captivity at Babylon in the second century. But this is merely a guess[1].

Before we quite part company with Sergius Paulus, the Pro-Consul of Cyprus, I should like to call your attention to one or two very curious coincidences which have strongly impressed my mind with the reality of the story in Acts xiii. You will remember that we read there that when Paul and Barnabas went to Cyprus, they found there a certain Jew named Barjesus, who was a sorcerer, or rather a magician (μάγος).

---

[1] Another instance is the application of the title of "King" to Herod Agrippa in Acts xii. 1, will be noticed later.

Now our first observation is that finding a Jewish magician in Cyprus, though the author of the Acts gives no explanation of it, was the most likely thing in the world, because Cyprus was the seat of a school of Jewish magicians said to have been founded by Moses and Jannes[1]. There was also a large Jewish population there. Our second observation is that Sergius Paulus is said to be "a man of understanding," R.V., and that this Jewish magician was with him as a part of his suite. What could this intelligent nobleman want with a Jewish magician? I think I can tell you. Sergius Paulus, besides being a Pro-Consul, was also an author, and one subject, if I mistake not, which had engaged his attention and employed his pen, as it afterwards did that of Pliny, was the history of magic. My reason for thinking so is that Pliny, in his great work on Natural History, prefixes to each book a list of the authors whom he has consulted for the contents of that book or chapter, and in two such lists the name of Sergius Paulus appears. Now, those two books (the second and eighteenth) contain notices, the one about eclipses, earthquakes, thunder and lightning, falling stars, prodigies of various kinds, auguries, prognostications, poisons, and

[1] Pliny, Hist. Natur. xxx. 1.

such like, which are subjects any work on magic would be likely to deal with (Lib. 11), and the other (Lib. xviii.) all kinds of observations and presages drawn from the appearance of the sun, the moon, the stars, thunder, the clouds, vapours, fires, water, and so on, subjects equally suitable for a work on magic. Bishop Lightfoot has also observed that in these two books of Pliny, for which Sergius Paulus is quoted, there is repeated mention of the island of Cyprus (appendix to Essays on Supernatural Religion), an account of the temple of Venus at Paphos, where rain never falls, and an account of corn grown in the island, from which black bread is made. Possibly Sergius Paulus's work embraced also some account of the island of Cyprus, of which he had been Governor, including a chapter on Jewish magic.

And now let us pass on to Ephesus. You will all remember the graphic account in Ch. xix. of the great riot at Ephesus caused by the Ephesian silversmiths, who felt their lucrative trade of making silver shrines for Diana to be in great danger by reason of the number of converts to the faith of Jesus Christ, made by the preaching of St. Paul. In the course of the description of this great uproar, which nearly cost St. Paul his life, we have attested the existence of the famous image of the goddess which fell down from Jupiter, the fanatical devotion of her worshippers, the magnificence of her shrine, and the widespread worship of her divinity, and the theatre as the place of public meeting. And as we read we seem to hear the tumultuous cry of ten thousand voices ringing through the air, Great is Diana of the Ephesians. Now, this description is in the strictest agreement with all the notices of the Diana of Ephesus contained in ancient historians, or found in inscriptions. "I swear by the great Ephesian Diana;" "the great goddess Diana;" "the very great goddess Diana;" "the Ephesian Diana, held by all men in the greatest honour;" are phrases which occur again and again. Inscriptions quite recently discovered at Ephesus[1] speak of the temples, statues, and altars everywhere consecrated to her, and of the solem assemblies held in her honour in the city of Ephesus, which is described as "the nurse of her own Ephesian goddess." In the same inscriptions the theatre appears as the recognised place of public assembly. Again, the "silver shrines" are small models in silver of the famous temple, with the image inside. They were used as a kind of phylactery or charm, carried about by travellers

[1] Wood's Ephesus.

to ensure their safety, or set up in houses. Such "shrines" of other goddesses are also mentioned, sometimes of gold, sometimes of silver, sometimes of terra cotta.

But we must not forget the distinctive names of Ephesian magistrates in this account. As Bishop Lightfoot observes, there are three distinct kinds of officers mentioned. There are the Pro-Consuls, the Town-Clerk, and the Asiarchs ($ἀνθύπατος$, $γραμματεύς$, and $Ἀσιάρχης$). Each of these is their proper and peculiar designation. Asia, of which Ephesus was the capital, being a Senatorial province, was ruled by a Pro-Consul; the Town-Clerk was an Ephesian officer who appears again and again in the Ephesian inscriptions. The Asiarchs, who also appear in the inscriptions, were the Presidents of the public games and religious ceremonials. They presided over the games of Pergamos and Smyrna as well as of Ephesus (all chief towns of the Roman province of Asia), whence their name of Asiarch. The agreement is singularly complete.

But we have not yet quite done with Ephesus. There are three words in the narrative of the Acts which deserve special notice. They all occur in the speech of the Town-Clerk (Acts xix. 35-39). The first is that in v. 35, translated "worshipper" in the A. V., "temple-keeper" in the R. V. (νεωκόρος). The word means literally "temple-sweeper." The *Neocoros* was a kind of sacristan or church-warden, whose business was especially to care for and regulate the worship of the god or goddess whose warden he was. The office might be held by an individual, but it was more commonly held by a city or community. In the corrupt times of the Roman Empire, from Nero downwards, it was considered a privilege to be the Neocoros of the reigning Roman Emperor, a privilege which was granted by the Senate, and was held frequently by the Ephesians, as appears on coins. But an inscription found at Ephesus some fifteen years ago actually has "the city of the Ephesians the Neocoros ... of Diana"—just as in the Acts. The next word is that in v. 37, (ἱεροσύλους) in the A. V. translated robbers of churches—better, of temples, in the R. V. One of the newly-discovered inscriptions found in the Theatre at Ephesus shows that this temple-robbing, or sacrilege, was a crime especially recognised by the Ephesian laws— "sacrilege (ἱεροσυλία) and profaneness" (the latter corresponding in sense to the "blasphemy" against the goddess in v. 39) are placed together as technical crimes. The Town-Clerk was talking in the strictly legal phraseology of his office. The third phrase is "a lawful assembly." This is also shown by the inscriptions to have been a technical phrase at Ephesus (νόμιμος and ἔννομος). I think you will be disposed to say *amen* to Bishop Lightfoot's dictum that "ancient literature has preserved no picture of the Ephesus of imperial times comparable for its life-like truthfulness to the narrative of St. Paul's sojourn there in the Acts." (Essays on Supernatural Religion, p. 301.)

And now we must hurry on to Thessalonica. In Acts xix. we read of St. Paul's visit to Thessalonica, and of his preaching the Gospel there. The unbelieving Jews, we are told, gathered a mob together and assaulted the house of Jason where St. Paul and Silas were lodging, with the intention of bringing them out to the people (δῆμος). But when they did not find them they laid hands on Jason and certain Christians whom they found there, and dragged them before the rulers of the city (τοὺς πολιτάρχας), and the same phrase, *Rulers of the City* is repeated in v. 8. Now there is nothing in this to attract the attention of an English reader; but when we turn to the Greek we find the phrase expressed by a single word "Politarchs." This word is found in no Greek writer, and the enquiry naturally arises what could induce the author of the Acts to make use of an unknown word to describe so simple a matter as the magistrates of the city? The answer to this enquiry can be given with absolute conclusiveness. Just as if I had been describing the annual dinner given by the Chief Magistrate of Bury St. Edmunds sixty years ago, at which I was present, I should have called him not (as he is now styled) the Mayor, but as he was then styled, the Alderman, of Bury; so the writer of the Acts calls the magistrates of the free city of Thessalonica Politarchs because that was their proper designation. More than a hundred years ago some old houses in Thessalonica (Salonica), which stood in front of one of the principal gateways of the city, were pulled down, and disclosed to view an ancient Greek inscription engraved on the marble arch, and in perfect preservation. The inscription, which I presume is intended to record the names of the persons who were Politarchs when the arch was erected, runs thus:—" When Sosipater, son of Cleopatra, Lucius Pontius Secundus, Polybius Flavius Sabinus, Demetrius son of Faustus, Demetrius son of Nicopolis, Zoilus son of Parmenius, otherwise called Meniscus, Gaius Agilleus Potitus, were Politarchs [1]." The archway is thought by some to have been erected between eighty and ninety years (B.C. 41–45) before St. Paul was at Thessalonica. Others place it some twenty years after St. Paul's visit. Anyhow, we have an indisputable proof that Politarch was the proper official designation of the Thessalonian Magistrates, just as the mention of the δῆμος in v. 5 (the people) is proper to a free Greek city such as Thessalonica was: and as, I may add, the mention of the Prætors (Magistrates A. V.) in v. 22, and of the lictors (serjeants) in v. 35 are proper to Philippi, a Roman colony, and would not be proper elsewhere.

Now when we recollect that all these minute agreements of the narrative with what we know to have been the state of things and persons at the time, and in the places, to which the narrative relates, are not the result of deep research on the part of the writer, but are involved in the simple recital of what was done day by day, we see at once that nothing can account for such agreement but the fact that the writer was an eye-witness of what he relates, and had before him, without any need for investigation, the

[1] It is also remarkable that three of these names, Sosipater, Secundus, and Gaius, are names of Macedonians who accompanied St. Paul.

facts and conditions of things, which we can now recover only by extensive learning, and the evidence of ancient coins, and the discovery of long buried inscriptions.

And now I must ask you to follow me to quite a different scene, the account given of Theudas in the speech of Gamaliel before the Jewish Sanhedrim in Acts v. Here there is a real difficulty and a wide discrepancy between the account in "the Acts" and the only other historical account we have of the same event, that namely in the Jewish historian, Josephus. Let us place the two accounts side by side. Gamaliel, as reported by the author of "the Acts," says: "Before these days rose up Theudas, boasting himself to be somebody, to whom a number of men, about 400, joined themselves, who was slain, and all, as many as obeyed him, were scattered and brought to nought. After this man rose up Judas of Galilee." (Acts v. 16.)

Josephus says, "When Fadus [1] was Procurator of Judea, a certain impostor, named Theudas, persuaded a great multitude of people to collect all their goods and chattels and follow him to

[1] The names Fadus and Varus (which last was the name of the Roman Procurator at the time when Luke places this incident) are very similar, almost identical if written in Aramean characters—וְדֻשׁ and וְרֻשׁ. This might have caused Josephus's mistake.

the river Jordan. For he said that he was a prophet, and promised to command the river to divide and afford an easy passage for them to the other side. With these words he deceived many. But Fadus did not allow them to reap any advantage from their folly; for he sent a troop of cavalry against them, which fell upon them suddenly, killed many of them, took many prisoners, and, having taken Theudas alive, cut off his head." (A. J. xx. v.)

Now I think these two accounts must relate to the same event. The same name of Theudas, the same character of an impostor, the same gathering of a multitude of followers deceived by his pretensions, and the same termination of the affair—the death of the leader, and the entire break up of his following—seem to mark decisively the identity of the two narratives. But Gamaliel fixes the time of Theudas' sedition before the "days of the taxing," i.e. before A.D. 6, whereas Josephus places it about A.D. 44, between thirty and forty years later. One of them then must be wrong. Is it Josephus? Or is it the author of the Acts? Now I would say, first, St. Luke is quite as good an authority as Josephus, to say the least. We have seen his wonderful accuracy in the instances (a few out of very many) which we have considered. Moreover, if Theudas' adventure happened when Josephus said it did, St. Luke must have remembered it. It was not twenty years before the time when he wrote the Acts. I do not think, therefore, that it is St. Luke who made the mistake. As we have no one else to appeal to, to decide, we must look at the internal evidence of the story itself, and see which time it fits best.

The time when Josephus places the incident was a time of perfect peace in Judea. The Jewish mind was unusually tranquil, and there was nothing to lead to such an undertaking as that of Theudas and his followers. It is quite out of place. But at the time where Gamaliel places the event, which would be just after Herod's death, Judea was in a state of turmoil—sedition followed sedition, pretenders of all kinds rose up, fire and sword were active in destruction all round. "Judea," says Josephus, "was full of lawless violence" (A. J. xvii. x. 8). And there came a new cause of agitation and disturbance. For the first time in its history Judea was threatened with being taxed by order of Augustus Cæsar. Josephus, A. J. xviii. i., tells us that at the first news of this taxation impending the Jews were indignant, and took it greatly to heart, though afterwards they were persuaded by the High Priest Joazar [1] to submit. Now it seems to me that the story of Theudas fits in here exactly. The question of the taxation of their goods, the sequel of the census taken before Herod's death (Luke ii. 1), was just being talked about, and was causing great agitation among the people. The impostor, Theudas, saw his opportunity. "Collect all your property [2], scrape together all the money you can, and come to me, and I will part the waters of the Jordan for you, and you will escape the grip of the tax-gatherer." And so under the fear of taxation the poor silly fellows flocked to Theudas and were killed by the Roman soldiers. The story suits the time exactly. I will just add that the submission of the Jews to the taxation did not last long. For when it was being enforced a few years after by Quirinius, the Roman Governor, the formidable rebellion of Judas of Galilee, to which Gamaliel alludes as following the adventures of Theudas, immediately ensued, and led to the untold misery of the Jewish people [3].

[1] Joazar was twice High Priest. The first time in the lifetime of Herod the Great.

[2] χρηματα, the same word as is used by Josephus xviii. 1, of the goods which the Jews allowed to be taxed under Quirinius.

[3] I shall revert to this subject of the taxing of Quirinius in my Fourth Lecture.

The next proof of the authenticity of the Acts, to which I will ask your attention, is that which has been so admirably handled by Paley in his *Horæ Paulinæ*. By the side of the history of St. Paul's life, which we have in " the Acts," we have also a collection of St. Paul's letters to the different Churches, which are mentioned in the Acts as founded or visited by him, as well as to certain individuals—Timothy, Titus, and Philemon. Paley's argument, which has never been refuted, is, that by comparing the two, the letters and the history, you can discover such a number of *undesigned coincidences*, as proves the authenticity both of the history and the letters. The whole strength of the argument lies in the coincidences being undesigned. He excludes, therefore, all those broad and palpable agreements which, though they must of course exist in real and genuine documents, yet might easily be managed by clever forgers, either fabricating letters to suit the history, or the history to suit the letters, or fabricating both; and confines his argument to such coincidences as are manifestly undesigned, and are proofs of truth underlying the statements in both documents. Thus he finds an undesigned confirmation of the statement in Acts xvi. 1, that Timothy's mother was a Jewess, in St. Paul's writing to him that "from a child he had known the Holy Scriptures" (2 Tim. iii. 15). And so with many other instances.

Now it is not necessary that I should go through the numerous examples in the *Horæ Paulinæ* of these undesigned coincidences which establish the truthfulness both of "the Acts" and of the Epistles. Paley's method is to go through each of the Epistles, and to show how casual phrases, and allusions, and statements in each Epistle exactly agree with what we read in "the Acts," in regard to facts, persons, chronology and localities; and that, in cases where the agreement is manifestly undesigned, and could not have been contrived either by a writer of the letters to make them agree with the history, or by a writer of the history to make it agree with the letters. Paley works out his argument with great ability, and the result seems to me to be that, if we are guided by evidence at all, we must believe that both the Epistles and the Acts are just what they pretend to be—the one the letters of the Apostles, the other a genuine contemporary history of the Apostle by one who knew him well.

I conclude, therefore, that we have in St. Paul's Epistles a contemporary testimony to the genuineness and trustworthiness of "the Acts of the Apostles." I ought, perhaps, here to add that there is one instance in which "the Acts" have been thought by some not to be in agreement with the Epistles. I mean as regards St. Paul's visit to Arabia immediately after his conversion. In the first chapter of the Epistle to the Galatians St. Paul says of himself that after his conversion he did not go up to Jerusalem to them that were Apostles before him, but went into Arabia, and returned again to Damascus. The account in the Acts makes no mention of St. Paul's visit to Arabia, but speaks of his preaching in the synagogues of Damascus, and increasing in strength. And then at v. 23 goes on to relate the conspiracy of the Jews to kill him, and his escape out of the city by being let down the city walls in a basket.

But when we come to look carefully at the different accounts we see that there is no sort of contradiction between them. We learn from the Epistle of St. Paul to the Galatians that three years elapsed between his conversion and his visit to Jerusalem (Gal. ii. 1). There was, therefore, abundant time for him to be at Damascus, and make a short stay there, and also to go into Arabia, and come back to Damascus, and tarry there a long while. And the narrative in the Acts distinctly favours the idea of two residences at Damascus, for in v. 19 we read that Saul "tarried certain days with the disciples which were at Damascus," an expression denoting a short time. But in v. 23 we read that "when many days were fulfilled (an expression, which as in 1 Kings ii. 38-39, may well denote two or three years) the Jews took counsel together to kill him." All then that we can say is either that the visit to Arabia had not been brought under the notice of the writer of "the Acts," or that he left it out as not being of importance to the point of view in which he was writing at the moment. His accuracy remains absolutely unimpeached.

There is another chapter in "the Acts," on the face of which, BY AN EYE-WITNESS, is written in such large, strong, unmistakable characters, that I must detain you a few minutes longer to lay some of its evidence before you. I mean the famous chapter of St. Paul's shipwreck on his voyage from Cæsarea to Rome in Acts xxvii., illustrated as it has been by the scarcely less famous commentary of Mr. Smith, of Jordan Hill. Of this last work, the latest edition, published just ten years ago, contains a preface by the present Bishop of Carlisle. In it he says that Dr. Whewell, then Master of Trinity College, Cambridge, speaking of Mr. Smith's work, told him that in his opinion no finer piece of demonstrative writing had appeared since the time of Paley, and Bishop Goodwin adds that he himself quite concurs with Dr. Whewell's estimate of the book. It is also interesting to me[1] to find that Mr. Smith was fully alive to the importance of the authenticity of the Acts, as a witness to the authenticity of the Gospel of St. Luke. For having observed that the writer of " the Acts " could not by any possibility have known what he records except by personal observation, he adds, " but if it can be shown that ' the Acts of the Apostles' are genuine and authentic, so must also be the Gospel, which is mentioned in that work, and is obviously by the same hand."

But to proceed, Mr. Smith, who was himself an experienced sailor, notices (p. 28) that the author of " the Acts " uses no fewer than thirteen different words to express the progress of a ship under different circumstances : to sail, to sail from a place, to sail across a sea, to sail slowly, to sail under a lee shore, and so on, and that in every instance he uses the right word with regard to the ship in which St. Paul was sailing, at the right moment, showing that the writer was in the ship at the time. He then marks that the

[1] I was not aware of this when I began these Lectures.

course the ship took, touching first at Sidon, and then keeping to the east and north of Cyprus, because the "winds were contrary," is in exact accordance with the testimony of English and French navigators as to the prevalence of strong west winds in those parts all through the summer. Again, the mention of Myra as the seaport on the coast of Lycia, where they found a ship of Alexandria, laden with corn, bound for Italy, and the size of the ship measured by the number of passengers, 276 souls (Acts xxvii. 37), is in exact accordance with what we know of Myra, as then a flourishing, populous, seaport, and of the ships of Alexandria, by which the corn trade between Egypt and Italy was carried on.

The voyage from Myra to "over against Cnidus" being exceedingly slow and laborious was doubtless caused by adverse winds; and when they came to the sea "over against Cnidus" the same wind made it impossible for them to proceed in the proper course for Italy. They should have sailed to the north of the island of Crete. But the wind made this impossible. They were consequently obliged to bear down to Salmone, and thence to coast along the south shore of the island as far as Fair Havens. Mr. Smith, with exact nautical knowledge, points out what the direction of the wind must have been to suit all these movements, viz. a N.W. wind; how, with such a wind, they could have reached Fair Havens, but, from the sudden trending of the shore northwards, could not have got further; he shows from many authorities that a N.W. wind is the wind which regularly prevails at that time of year, and gives remarkable parallel cases of ships, including some English ones under command of Admiral Saumarez, being obliged by contrary winds to keep to the south of Crete, instead of sailing to the north as they intended. Moreover Fair Havens (a small bay still so-called in Greek—καλὸι λιμένες) and the ruins of the city of Lasea, three miles off, and the harbour of Phœnice (Lutro [1]) and the island of Clauda (now called Gozzo), have been identified, and are situated exactly where they ought to be according to the narrative in the Acts; and the moderate breeze from the south was just what would enable them to sail close along the Cretan shore. They were making, you will remember, for the harbour of Phœnice (or Phœnix R.V.), on the western end of Crete, where they hoped to winter in safety.

[1] Some doubt is thrown upon the identification of Lutro in the Dictionary of the Bible—"Phenice"; in the R. V. more correctly Phœnix.

But to reach it they had to pass a bit of open sea for about 34 miles. They had not, however, proceeded far before a sudden typhoon from the N.E. sprung up with such violence that the ship could not face it, but was obliged to scud before it. They were driven down to the south of the island of Clauda. Here, under shelter of the island, the water was comparatively smooth, and they were able to perform two important operations. One was to hoist the boat on board, and the other was to undergird, or frap, the ship, i. e. to pass a strong cable three or four times round the hull of the ship, so as to ease her straining [1]. It is probable that she had already begun to spring a leak from the violence of the waves, and, had it not been for this precaution, would probably soon have foundered. The next danger was of being driven by the N.E. [2] wind upon "the quicksand," better rendered in the R.V. "the Syrtis," i.e. a very dangerous reach of sea and sands on the northern coast of Africa, full of shallows and sunken rocks. To avoid this they "lowered the gear," i. e. probably the spars and rigging, and heavy yards, set the storm-sail,

---

[1] Mr. Smith gives several instances of this operation in modern times. But it was common in ancient navigation. See Smith's Dissertation on the Ships of the Ancients.

[2] E. N. E. exactly.

and, Smith says, proceeded on the star-board tack, going as near the wind as possible, which was their only chance of avoiding the Syrtis. Under these circumstances their course would bring them straight to Malta, a distance of 476 miles, which they neared on the fourteenth night, the exact time which, under the circumstances, the voyage should have taken. Passing over other characteristic incidents, such as the throwing the cargo and the tackling overboard to lighten the damaged ship, the counting the number of passengers, and so on, I will only notice, in the last place, the final shipwreck on the coast of Malta. Here all the circumstances mentioned in the Acts agree with astonishing minuteness with what must have happened to a ship in the immediate neighbourhood of St. Paul's Bay at Malta under the circumstances described. The first warning of the approach to land, doubtless the breakers seen or heard breaking upon the rocky point of Koura; the exact depth of the successive soundings, 20, and then 15 fathoms; the low, flat nature of that part of the island which prevented its being seen at a distance; the excellent anchorage, the rocks, the anchors cast out at the stern, and then afterwards cut away and left in the sea; the loosing the rudder, which had been secured by lashings while the ship was at anchor; the hoisting the foresail, the creek with a shore, the place where two seas meet, the muddy, clayey bottom in which the fore-part of the ship stuck, while the stern was battered by the waves; these are all shown to be in minute agreement with the actual condition of that part of the island, and with the conduct which good seamanship would have dictated under the circumstances. When I have added that other details, such as the conduct of the sailors in trying to escape by the boat till prevented by the soldiers; the advice of the soldiers to kill the prisoners lest they should escape; the consistent kindness of the Centurion to St. Paul; the further voyage from Malta to Puteoli, and the journey from thence to Rome; are no less true to nature and to fact than those which we have been considering, I conclude without the smallest hesitation that you may be as certain as that you are sitting there that the man who wrote the account of St. Paul's voyage from Cæsarea to Rome, which we have in Acts xxvii. and xxviii., was in the ship with the Apostle, and tells us, not what he learnt from others, but what he saw with his own eyes, and experienced in his own person.

And here I must stop to-night. In our next

Lecture we shall first complete what we have to say about "the Acts," especially by proving that the author whom we have hitherto treated as unknown, was St. Luke, and by showing what was the date of his work. This we shall do from the internal evidence of "the Acts," assisted by St. Paul's Epistles.

I shall then hope to begin the examination of the authenticity of the Gospel of St. Luke, which our previous work will have made easy and conclusive.

LIST OF BOOKS CHIEFLY USED IN THE FOREGOING LECTURE.

Bishop Lightfoot's Essays on Supernatural Religion.
Dean Plumptre's Commentary on the Acts of the Apostles in Bishop Ellicott's Commentary.
Lewin's Life and Epistles of St. Paul.
Conybeare and Howson's Life and Epistles of St. Paul.
Paley's Horæ Paulinæ.
Josephus' Jewish Antiquities.
Pulpit Commentary on Acts of the Apostles.
Voyage and Shipwreck of St. Paul.—Smith of Jordan Hill.

LECTURE III.

PART I.

In my first Lecture I showed you the importance of being able to prove that the Gospels are the works of contemporaries of the events narrated in them. I then pointed out that the evidence of this is of two kinds:—(1) The external evidence—(2) The internal evidence; and that the concurrence of these two kinds of evidence must command our assent. I gave you some reasons for my selection of the Gospel of St. Luke, and dwelt upon the supreme importance of ascertaining the genuineness of the "Acts of the Apostles" in consequence of the testimony it bears in its first verse to that Gospel.

In pursuance of this object we went on to consider the external testimony to the authenticity of the "Acts of the Apostles," and that completed our first Lecture.

In my second Lecture I went into some of the internal evidences. We tested the accuracy of the writer in respect of his historical notices

of persons and places; we tried his accuracy
and truth by the parallel authority of St. Paul's
Epistles, as carried out by Paley in his *Horæ
Paulinæ*; and lastly, under the guidance of Mr.
Smith, of Jordan Hill, we examined the narrative
of St. Paul's shipwreck, subjecting it to the test
of nautical science, of scientific navigation, of
meteorology, of topology, and of recent experience
in the same seas. In each of these departments
the accuracy of the writer was found to be absolutely faultless.

We are to follow up the subject this evening
by finding out from the book itself, aided by
St. Paul's Epistles, what was the name of this
charming writer, who secures our confidence
by his accuracy, and engages our interest by his
animated and picturesque descriptions.

The first step in this enquiry is to notice that
it appears distinctly that the writer, during a
portion of the events which he relates, was
present, and took part in what was being done.
We learn this with absolute certainty from what
are called the *we* passages in "the Acts." In
those passages the writer, instead of saying *they*
did so and so, says, "*We* did so and so." This
change first occurs, Acts xvi. 10, on occasion of
St. Paul's visit to Europe, showing that the
writer was then at Troas, and ceases when at

Philippi. It occurs again in Acts xx. 5, when St. Paul, on his return from Corinth, and on his way to Jerusalem, went to Philippi at the time of the Passover. There the writer of the Acts joined him, because in mentioning that certain other of St. Paul's companions preceded him to Asia, he says, " These waited for *us* at Troas, and *we* sailed away from Philippi after the days of unleavened bread, and came unto them to Troas in five days, where *we* tarried seven days." And if you will look at the following chapters you will see by this same sign that the writer accompanied Paul to Mitylene, and Miletus, and Cos, and Rhodes, and Tyre ; that he was of the company at that touching scene when the Tyrian Christians, with their wives and children, accompanied Paul and his party to the sea-shore, when, as he says, " *We* kneeled down on the shore and prayed : and when *we* had taken leave of one another *we* went on board the ship, but they returned home again." And then the narrative goes on showing that the writer was still with St. Paul at Ptolemais and Cæsarea, and at length reached Jerusalem, and was with him at his reception by James (xxi. 18) and all the elders of the Church of Jerusalem. We have no direct evidence of the presence of the writer with St. Paul during the next two years, but we have indirect evidence in the very circumstantial and detailed accounts of the doings and speeches of the Apostle in chapters xxi–xxvi. And so when we find the *we* again in chapter xxvii. 1 and following verses, it is natural to conclude that the writer had been with St. Paul all the time of his being a prisoner at Cæsarea.

Well, when the eventful day came, and St. Paul sailed from Cæsarea as a prisoner to make his appeal to Cæsar, the Emperor Nero, at Rome, the writer of the Acts sailed with him. "When it was determined that *we* should sail into Italy ... entering into a ship of Adramyttium, *we* launched," &c. (Acts xxvii. 1). That he was in the ship with the Apostle all through the disastrous voyage to Malta we saw clearly enough in our last Lecture. And if we turn to Acts xxviii. 2, we shall see that he left Malta with him in the "Castor and Pollux," and went on to Syracuse, and thence to Puteoli, the seaport of Campania, to which ships from Alexandria, laden with corn for the Roman market, habitually came (Seneca, Ep. 79). After tarrying there seven days with the little Christian community which they found there, they proceeded to Rome, where Paul remained for two years. And then all the positive information to be got from "the Acts" ceases.

We must not, however, forget to notice that "the Acts" gives negative evidence as to which of St. Paul's companions did not write "the Acts." It was not Sopater, or Aristarchus the Thessalonian, or Secundus, or Gaius, or Timothy, or Tychicus, or Trophimus, because these are all mentioned in xx. 4 as having gone to Troas, while the writer of "the Acts" tarried with St. Paul at Philippi. Neither, we may add with equal confidence, was it Silas, who is not mentioned in connection with St. Paul's later journeys, not after Acts xviii. 5, who does not appear at all at Rome, and who moreover is distinctly a different person from the writer, who in xv. 22 describes him as "a chief man among the brethren." Then the "we" form does not appear at times when we know that Silas was with St. Paul (Acts xvii. 14, 15), so that we may dismiss the hypothesis of Silas being the author, seeing it has such decisive proofs against it, and absolutely nothing in its favour.

Who then was the writer? The writer, whoever he was, came with St. Paul to Rome, and stayed there during two years. Now during those two years St. Paul wrote several letters. In fact four: Ephesians, Philippians, Colossians, and Philemon. In two of these there are no salutations by name. But in the two others,

Colossians and Philemon, we find salutations sent by St. Paul's companions. Thus in Colossians iv. 14, among other salutations, we read, "Luke, the beloved physician, and Demas greet you." And in Philemon: "Marcus, Aristarchus, Demas, and Luke, salute thee."

Here then we have important information. We learn for certain that Luke was at Rome with St. Paul, with St. Paul's other "companions in travel," xix. 29. But we learn much more. We learn that he was specially loved by St. Paul. He had endeared himself to the Apostle by long and tried service, by faithful, devoted attachment, by companionship in labour and peril. Assume that it was he who never left him in that trying time at Jerusalem, who gave up everything that he might cheer his two years' confinement at Cæsarea, who was his companion in that memorable shipwreck in the Adriatic, who was now by his side in his prison at Rome, and what significance it gives to the epithet "the beloved." Assuredly Luke, "the beloved Physician," was no new friend of St. Paul's, and had anybody but Luke himself been the historian of St. Paul's life and labours, Luke's name would have been prominent in the history.

Again, from the place in which Luke's name stands among the salutations in Coloss. iv., we learn that he was a Gentile by birth; for after enumerating several, whom he describes as "of the circumcision," he passes on to Epaphras, Luke, and Demas, whence it is obvious to infer that these were not of the circumcision. Now the Gospel of St. Luke and the Acts both contain many indications that the writer was a Gentile. The dedication to "the most excellent Theophilus," a Gentile of high rank; the general tone of the Gospel dwelling on the universality of God's Grace as embracing Jew and Gentile alike; the very genealogy of Christ not stopping, like St. Matthew's, at Abraham, but going up to Adam, the father of the whole human race; and, generally, the language, indicating a Greek and not a Jewish writer; the attachment of the writer to St. Paul, " the Apostle of the Gentiles," and the special interest taken by him in the conversion of the Gentiles, whether by St. Peter (Acts x.) or St. Paul, all agree with the hypothesis of the writer being himself a Gentile.

Again, we are told by St. Paul that Luke was a "Physician." Now that necessarily implies a man of liberal education: accordingly we find the Gospel of St. Luke and the Acts of the Apostles written in very good classical Greek, and in an excellent style.

But to crown all. If the writer of " the Acts "

was a Physician we should expect to find some traces of it in his writing. If a military man writes a book you are pretty sure to find some military phrases in it. An artist will introduce words or ideas connected with art, a theologian cannot quite throw off his theological language, and a lawyer will betray his legal training, and show his accurate legal knowledge as occasion may arise. If then the writer of "the Acts" (to confine ourselves for the moment to "the Acts") was a well-educated physician, acquainted with all the best medical writers, and familiar with all the terms of medical science, it will be sure to show itself in his book. Are there any signs in "the Acts of the Apostles" that the writer was a physician? Well, there are in "the Acts" alone 233 words which are distinctly medical terms, not all of them of course exclusively so, but all of them words specially used by medical writers, and most of them words which occur nowhere else in the New Testament but in St. Luke's Gospel and in the Acts of the Apostles. The number of such words in St. Luke's Gospel is 252, in all 485. Now whatever exception may be taken to some of these words as not necessarily medical, I do not think it can be denied that the employment of nearly 500 words, much used in medical works, and habitually employed by such writers as Hippocrates, Aretæus, Galen, and Dioscorides, is a most striking confirmation of the hypothesis that the writer was a physician, and is a crowning evidence of the authorship of St. Luke, which was the unanimous testimony of Christian antiquity [1].

The following examples, selected from "Hobart's Medical Language of St. Luke," will enable you to judge for yourselves. In Acts i. 3, the writer says that our Lord showed Himself alive after His Passion "by many *infallible proofs*," in Greek, τεκμηρίοις. Now this word τεκμήριον (tecmerion) only occurs in this one place in the N.T. But it is a word in frequent use among medical writers to express the *infallible symptoms* of a disease in opposition to σημεῖα (semeia), signs which are doubtful. It is so defined, and so used very frequently, by Galen, Hippocrates, and Aretæus.

In Acts i. 4, the word *wait* is expressed in the Greek by a word found nowhere else in the N.T., περιμένειν (perimencin). It means "to wait in

---

[1] The evidence from medical terms in the Gospel and "the Acts," and from the coincidence of Luke's visits to St. Paul with times of more than usual infirmity in the Apostle, is well brought out in the Introduction to St. Luke's Gospel by Dean Plumptre in Bishop Ellicott's New Testament Commentary.

expectation of what is to follow," and is in frequent use by medical writers to mean "waiting for the result of some medicine, or medical treatment."

Acts i. 18. "Headlong" πρηνής (prenes), found nowhere else in the N.T. A technical word in medical writers.

Acts xix. 29. "Confusion" σύγχυσις (synchysis), found nowhere else in N.T. Of very frequent use in medical writers for a general "disturbance of the system."

Acts ii. 13. "New wine" γλεῦκος (gleucos). Nowhere else in the N.T. Of frequent use by medical writers in speaking of the kind of wine they prescribed for their patients. *Ib.* "Full" μεμεστωμένοι (memestomenoi). Nowhere else to be found in the N.T.; but used by medical writers.

Acts iii. 4. "Fastening his eyes" ἀτενίσας (atenisas)—used twelve times in Luke and Acts, and elsewhere in N.T. only 2 Cor. iii. 7–13—is the medical term denoting a peculiar, fixed look, Hippocrates, Aretæus, Galen. *Ib.* "The restitution of all things" ἀποκατάστασις (apocatastasis). Nowhere else in the N.T. The regular medical word for "complete recovery" of health in body or limb.

Acts iv. 17. "Spread" διανέμεσθαι (dianemesthai). Only here in the N.T. It is the favourite medical word for the diffusion or distribution of food, of blood, of the nerves, &c., over the whole body. The same is true of two other words used only by St. Luke, viz. $διεσ$-$πάρησαν$ (diesparesan), "scattered abroad," Acts viii. 1, 4, &c., and "delivered," $ἀναδόντες$ (anadontes), Acts xxiii. 33. They were favourite medical terms. The following words also: "healing" $ἴασις$ (iasis), iv. 22; "ran together" $συνδρομή$ (syndrome), xxi. 30; "concourse" $συστροφή$ (systrophe), Acts xix. 40; "The hearing," (decision R.V.) $διάγνωσις$ (diagnosis), xxv. 21; with many others, are technical medical terms, and found only in St. Luke.

Acts x. 11. "A great sheet knit at the four corners." The words for "sheet" $ὀθόνη$ (othone), and for "corners," $ἀρχαί$ (archai), are both peculiar to St. Luke. They are also the technical and exclusive medical terms for a linen bandage and its ends. This is a very striking example, and there are many more nearly as striking.

I will only add that it is in St. Luke's Gospel alone that we find the record of the Proverb—Physician, heal thyself (Luke iv. 23).

It may be worth just adding that the authorship of the Gospel and the Acts must have been notorious when they first appeared, because, though St. Luke did not attach his name to them, Theophilus knew very well who wrote them and who sent them to him, and would naturally be proud to communicate this knowledge to all his fellow-Christians around him, so that the knowledge of the authorship would be the common property of the whole Church from the time of the first appearance of the works.

I think, then, that I may now say, without any unseemly confidence, that we have not only proved the authenticity of "the Acts of the Apostles" and the marvellous accuracy of the writer by every test that could be applied to him, but that we have also placed it beyond all reasonable doubt that the writer was St. Luke, the physician, and companion of St. Paul, as all antiquity unanimously affirms. Consequently henceforth instead of using the periphrasis " the author of the Acts," I shall call the author by the name of Luke, with as much confidence as I ascribe the History of England to Lord Macaulay, or that of the Norman Conquest to Mr. Freeman.

But there is one more important service that " the Acts of the Apostles " must do us before we pass on to the Gospel, and that is to determine the chronology. I mean the time of the publication of Luke's Gospel.

You will all remember that the book of "the Acts" ends with the following words (R.V.), " He abode two whole years in his own hired dwelling, and received all that went in unto him preaching the Kingdom of God, and teaching the things concerning the Lord Jesus Christ with all boldness, none forbidding him." And there St. Luke stops. Not a word about St. Paul's appearing before Nero; about his being set at liberty, about his journey to Spain, or any of the subsequent events of his life, which it would have been so deeply interesting to the Church to be acquainted with. How can we account for this? We can only account for it reasonably in one way, a way which is obvious and natural, and does thoroughly account for it, viz. that Luke published his history at this time, before anything else had happened. I conceive that he put his notes into shape at Rome during St. Paul's imprisonment. He had probably been collecting materials for his history for some time past. While at Jerusalem he would have learnt from James, and from other persons, those events which are related in the early chapters of "the Acts," and of which St. Paul was only partially cognizant. He would have learnt from St. Paul's own lips much about Stephen, and the persecution, and his own conversion; and from Timothy, and other of St. Paul's companions, many particulars about which St. Paul may have been reticent. He would have made full notes of the things that passed under his own eyes from the time when he permanently joined the Apostle's company : taken down St. Paul's speeches from the stairs of the Castle, before the Sanhedrim, before Felix and Festus, and so on; prepared the account of the shipwreck, taken down St. Paul's speeches to the Jews in his hired house at Rome, and then employed his leisure at Rome in putting it altogether as we now read it in "the Acts." And then came the sudden order for St. Paul to appear before his judges—the trial, the liberation, the departure from Rome. All then would be bustle and confusion; there was no more literary leisure. So the finished work was sent off to Theophilus, perhaps with the intention, which was never realised, of adding another chapter at some future time.

Anyhow, it seems to me quite certain that the date of "the Acts of the Apostles" is fixed by that of the last event recorded in the book.

Now we know from Roman history that Festus became Procurator of Judæa in the course of A.D. 60. And as Paul was at Cæsarea for a time after the arrival of Festus, and was delayed several months by his shipwreck, and was two years a prisoner at Rome, and as the Acts of the Apostles were not published till the end of those two years, we get the year A.D. 63 for the publication of "the Acts." And, as Dean Alford says, we thus get a fixed date, before which the Gospel of St. Luke must have been written. And that must suffice us for the present.

PART II.

We now proceed to the main purpose of our lectures, which is to establish the authenticity of the Gospel according to St. Luke. And it might be enough to say that St. Luke in the very first verse of "the Acts," which we have now proved to be authentic, tells us plainly that he had written a Gospel. "The former treatise have I made, O Theophilus, of all that Jesus began both to do and teach, until the day that He was taken up" (Acts i. 1, 2). And I think no one who has not an unusually big bump of scepticism could manage to get up a suspicion that our Gospel of St. Luke is not the "treatise" of which St. Luke there speaks.

Still, as there is never any harm in having two or three strings to one's bow, it will be well to spend a quarter of an hour in showing what further internal evidence there is that the Gospel of St. Luke is by the same author as "the Acts of the Apostles."

I. Even the most sceptical writers, such as Rénan and Dr. Davidson, acknowledge that the authors of the third Gospel, and of "the Acts of the Apostles," are one and the same person. "The identity of the writer (of 'Acts') with the third Evangelist is undoubted," says Davidson, "because the diction and style of both is the same." (Vol. ii. p. 145.) And he proceeds to enumerate some 46 words, "not fewer than 50" (Dean Plumptre on "Acts," in Commentary for Schools, p. 1), which are found both in the Gospel of St. Luke and in "the Acts of the Apostles," but are found nowhere else in the New Testament. Moreover the general style in both works is the same. The Greek is more classical than in the other Gospels; the thought is simple and lucid, and the historical spirit of the writer is apparent in both works. There is in both works the same spirit of research, the same habit of mind seeking out, and narrating distinctly, the deep springs and causes of the things narrated, which belongs to the clear-minded historian. Compare, e. g., the first chapter of St. Luke's Gospel with the first chapter of "the Acts." You see in both how carefully the foundations of the future narrative are laid. And so with regard to Peter's mission to Cornelius, the foundation of the Church at Antioch, the mission of Paul and Barnabas to the heathen, we see a certain thoroughness in tracing the beginnings and the details of things which meets us also in the Gospel. Look again at St. Luke's account of the seventy, at the account of the quarrel and reconciliation of Pontius Pilate and Herod, the penitence of the thief on the cross, and other instances of original historical investigation such as we have seen in "the Acts of the Apostles." The same historical instinct shows itself in marking the chronology by the reign or the government under which the events occurred. Thus Luke i. 5, we read: "There was in the days of Herod, King of Judæa, a certain Priest." Luke ii. 1, 2: "There went out a decree from Cæsar Augustus." . . . "When Quirinius was Governor of Syria." Luke iii. 1: "In the fifteenth year of the reign of Tiberius Cæsar, Pontius Pilate being Governor of Judæa, and Herod being Tetrarch of Galilee, &c., in the High Priesthood of Annas and Caiaphas, the Word of God came to John the son of Zacharias," &c. The historian wants his readers to know the exact time when the things which he relates happened. And so in " the Acts of the Apostles," the imprisonment and rescue of St. Peter is fixed to just before the death of King Herod Agrippa; St. Paul's visit to Corinth came just after the Emperor Claudius had banished the Jews from Rome; Claudius Lysias was in command of the garrison of Jerusalem when St. Paul was assaulted by a Jerusalem mob; Felix was governor when he was sent to Cæsarea; Festus had succeeded Felix when he was sent as a prisoner to Rome. Here you have the same historical exactness. The events are not related at random, unconnected with the secular history of the times, but they are defined and fixed as to time and place by historical dates, and accurate topography. In a word the same spirit in the two books shows that they are both by the hand of the same author.

I must refer too once more to the same medical language in the two works. The existence of 233 medical terms in "the Acts of the Apostles," against 252 in the Gospel of St. Luke, is an unmistakable evidence of identical authorship. You will observe that I use this argument now not to prove that the author was a physician (though it does this), but in confirmation of the fact that he who wrote "the Acts" had before written the Gospel. Perhaps one or two examples will help to make this clearer to your minds. In Acts xxviii. 8, we read that "Publius *lay sick* of a fever." In Luke iv. 38, that "Simon's wife's mother was *taken with* a great fever." In the Greek the phrase is identical (συνεχόμενος, sunechomenos), and the language strictly medical. In Matthew and Mark the same miracle is recorded but in different phraseology.

Take again Luke vi. 18: "They that were *vexed* with unclean spirits," and Acts v. 16: "Sick folks and them that were *vexed* with unclean spirits." The Greek word for "vexed," ὀχλούμενοι (ochloumenoi), occurs only in these two places in the New Testament, but is employed very frequently indeed by medical writers to express being *vexed* or *troubled* by any pain or sickness.

One more example shall suffice. In Luke vii. 15, we read of the young man at Nain, that at the word of Jesus he that was dead "*sat up* and began to speak"; and again Acts ix. 40, we read of Dorcas, that when Peter, turning to the dead body, said, "Tabitha, arise," she opened her eyes and *sat up*. The Greek word (ἀνεκάθισεν) here rendered *sat up* occurs nowhere else in the New Testament besides these two places, but is the regular word in medical writings for a patient *sitting up*.

It would be easy to multiply such examples, which show very clearly that the Gospel of St. Luke and the Acts of the Apostles were written by the same person, thus confirming the direct testimony of Acts i. 1. But it is needless to pursue the subject further.

II. Another very palpable evidence of identity of authorship in the two books is obtained by comparing the close of the Gospel with the beginning of "the Acts." We see there something like the indentures of legal deeds, where the way in which the indented edge of one parchment fits into the indented edge of the other, shows that they are parts of the same deed. If you look at the close of the Gospel and the beginning of "the Acts" you will see that the same thoughts which ended the one were still working in the commencement of the other. The historian of the Church is careful to connect the history, which is to follow, with the last days on earth of the Divine Founder of the Church. He recapitulates, and in recapitulating enlarges and adds to, the circumstances of our Lord's last intercourse with His disciples, which he had related in the Gospel. He reverts to the infallible proofs of the Lord's Resurrection, His being handled by the disciples, and eating with them, which he had there recorded (Luke xxiv. 29-43); he gives more fully the Lord's words concerning that outpouring of the Holy Spirit, which was to form so striking a feature of the ensuing narrative, and reiterates our Lord's command to them to tarry at Jerusalem till they received the promise of the Father. For all this was essential to that description of the attitude of the Church after the ascension of Christ, with which the history of "the Acts of the Apostles" properly begins at the twelfth verse. In more than one instance the very words of the Gospel are repeated in "the Acts" with amplification. Thus Luke xxiv. 48, it is said, "Ye are witnesses of these things;" while Acts i. 8, we read, "Ye shall be witnesses unto me both in Jerusalem, and in all Judea, and in Samaria, and unto the uttermost part of the earth." In Luke xxiv. 49, it is said, "I send the promise of my Father upon you." In Acts i. 4, "Wait for the promise of the Father which ye heard of me," with the explanation following, "For John indeed baptized with water, but ye shall be baptized with the Holy Ghost not many days hence." In Luke xxiv. 52, "They returned to Jerusalem." In Acts i. 12, "Then returned they to Jerusalem." The two accounts, you see, dovetail into one another. You could not fit the first chapter of "the Acts" to the close of the Gospels of St. Matthew, St. Mark, or St. John, in the same way.

III. Another indication of the identity of the writers of St. Luke's Gospel and "the Acts of the Apostles" may be seen in the very similar way in which they both quote Scripture, and give at length the speeches or songs of the personages introduced. In St. Luke's Gospel look at the Magnificat, the Benedictus, the Nunc Dimittis, all given at full length; compare the long quotation from Isaiah in Luke iii. 4, 5, 6, with the short ones in the parallel passages in Matthew, Mark, and John; see the full quotation from Isaiah lxi. 1, 2; and other more or less conspicuous examples; and then turn to "the Acts." There you have, in chapter i., Peter's address; his sermon, with the long quotation from Joel, in chapter ii.; and another from the Psalms in the same chapter; another from the second Psalm in chapter iv.; the speech of Gamaliel in chapter v.; the long speech of Stephen, full of quotations, in chapter vii.; the quotation from Isaiah liii. in chapter viii.; the speech of

Peter in chapter x.; the speech of Paul at Antioch in Pisidia; the speeches of Peter and James at the Council of Jerusalem; the speech of Paul at Athens, at Miletus, and his memorable apologies before the people at Jerusalem, before the Sanhedrim, before Felix, and before Festus and Agrippa; all given at full length; and the final quotation from Isaiah in his remonstrance with the Jews at Rome. All this shows the same habit of mind pervading the Gospel and the Acts, and so falls in with other indications of identity of authorship.

IV. One other indication of identity of authorship has struck me, which, however, I lay before you with some hesitation, because I do not feel sure that it is real. I must ask you, therefore, to accept it as in some measure conjectural and possibly unsound, and to take it for what it is worth, and no more. If it will not bear sober criticism you may throw it aside. We do not need it, because our evidence is already conclusive. If it does not strengthen our evidence, at all events it does not weaken it. It is simply not to the purpose.

In reading the early chapters of "the Acts of the Apostles" everybody must be struck with the prominent place given to St. Peter. He takes the lead in the first joint action of the

Church in the election of an apostle in the room of Judas, and his address to the Church is given at length. It is he who stands up with the Eleven on the day of Pentecost and delivers that striking discourse which fills up so large a part of the second chapter. In the three following chapters, and in chapter viii., though John is mentioned by his side, it is still Peter who says and does everything that is recorded. In the ninth, tenth, and eleventh chapters it is still Peter whose great figure fills up the foreground of the canvas, and whose sayings and doings are recorded by St. Luke. And chapter xii. is devoted to his imprisonment and deliverance by the angel. See, too, chapter xv. Well! This is no doubt owing to the place Peter filled in the Church by our Lord's appointment. But still we can hardly suppose that St. John and the other apostles said and did nothing worth recording, that they were mere dummies in the great Church drama that was being acted. Can there have been any other reason—a secondary one, but still an influential one—for this very marked prominence given by St. Luke to Peter in the first twelve chapters of "the Acts"?

If you turn to the xxiind chapter of St. Luke's Gospel, from verse 54 to verse 62, you will there find a full and elaborate account of Peter's denial of Christ. The story is told with that simplicity and straightforwardness which characterizes the Gospel narratives; but it was a very painful story for a brother Christian to tell. *We* read of it more than eighteen centuries after the actor and the narrator have been laid in their graves. I do not think it ever occurred to me before to consider how Peter would like the tale of his weakness to be proclaimed through all the Churches in the world, or how Luke would like to be the historian of that weakness. But if we would appreciate the circumstances truly, we must remember that at the time of the publication of Luke's Gospel Peter was alive, actively fulfilling the duties of his Apostolate. Luke had probably met him frequently and known him well at Jerusalem, at Antioch or elsewhere. He well knew the high place which Peter filled in the Church of God, and the love and reverence with which he was regarded by Christians everywhere. What then could be more painful or more irksome to him than the stern duty imposed upon him of recording so sad a blot upon a saintly life. St. John had the opportunity of following up his narrative of Peter's denial by the touching story in his xxi[st] chapter of our Lord's tender committal to Peter's care of the sheep of His flock, and of Peter's passionate asseveration of his love to his Divine Master. Is it not very probable that having faithfully recorded Peter's denial in his history of Christ, Luke should now take every opportunity of magnifying the name of the penitent and forgiven servant in his history of the Church, and showing how worthily he had fulfilled the arduous duties of his Apostolic office?

It is, perhaps, some corroboration of this view that St. Luke has not recorded in "the Acts" an incident, of which he must have been aware, viz. that at Antioch Peter had again conducted himself with such weakness and want of moral courage as to draw down upon himself that severe rebuke from St. Paul, of which he speaks in Galat. ii. 11 : "When Peter was come to Antioch, I withstood him to the face, because he was to be blamed." If he was not obliged, by historical faithfulness, to record this incident, we can understand that he would prefer to omit it.

And here, I think, we may conveniently break off for to-night. The point to which I have conducted you, as I hope safely and surely, is that "the Acts of the Apostles" is beyond all reasonable doubt the work of St.

Luke, " the beloved Physician," the friend and companion of St. Paul; that " the former treatise," to which he alludes in the first verse of that work, is " the Gospel according to St. Luke"; and that there is strong internal evidence that the two works proceeded from the same pen. I will ask you to think over what has been said on each of these heads, and to make up your minds decisively one way or the other, just as if you were on a jury, whether the evidence adduced is satisfactory and conclusive or not. My object in these Lectures is not merely a literary one, to establish the authorship of these books as one would establish the authenticity of a work of Tacitus, or a play of Shakespeare, but to show you that in believing what you read in them with an unshaken and undoubting faith, you are resting upon solid ground, and are accepting as truth that which will carry you safely through all the trials and difficulties of life, and will not fail you either in the hour of death or at the great day of judgment.

Our next Lecture will examine the proofs of the authenticity of the Gospel, irrespective of " the Acts of the Apostles."

LIST OF BOOKS CHIEFLY USED IN THE FOREGOING LECTURE.

Paley's Horæ Paulinæ.
Alford's Commentary of the New Testament.
Hobart's Medical Language of St. Luke.
Introduction to St. Luke's Gospel by Dean Plumptre in Ellicott's Commentary of the New Testament.
Dr. Davidson's Introduction to the Study of the New Testament.
Commentary for Schools—St. Luke's Gospel by Dean Plumptre.

LECTURE IV.

In our Lecture to-night we are to consider the proofs of the authenticity of the Gospel according to St. Luke, irrespective of "the Acts of the Apostles." It is quite true that if our previous reasoning has been sound, that authenticity has been already proved, and we really require no further evidence. At the same time, as further evidence does exist, and as the examination of it contributes a good deal to our understanding and appreciation of the Gospel itself, I do not think our time and attention will be thrown away if we devote an hour this evening to the consideration of it.

We will first look at the writer's description of his own work in his opening words (Luke i. 1–4). He tells us that when he undertook to write his Gospel there already existed many narratives by different hands of the things most surely believed (or, as some render it, most thoroughly authenticated) among Christians, in accordance with what had been reported to them by those who from the first had been eye-witnesses and ministers of the Word. He does not say that these narratives were incorrect, nor does he enable us to judge certainly whether either of the other synoptic Gospels was included in this number, though I rather think they were not. But he shows plainly that he did not think anything already written was exhaustive or complete; and that he was in possession of much additional matter which had not yet been circulated among Christians, but which it would be profitable for them to know. Accordingly, having had special opportunities of acquiring accurate knowledge of the whole Gospel history from its very beginning, he had determined to draw up a more complete and orderly account for the benefit of his friend and patron Theophilus, who hitherto had derived his knowledge of Christian truth from oral tradition and catechetical instruction alone (*which thou wert taught by word of mouth.*—R.V. margin). And here it may be well to observe that for the first twenty or thirty years of the existence of the Church, Christians had to depend upon oral instruction alone. There were no written Gospels. The structure of the three synoptic Gospels shows distinctly, as is well brought out in Professor Norton's book, that the teaching of the Apostles was oral; that by degrees this teaching repeated over and over again became stereotyped, whence the verbal agreement in so many passages of the synoptic Evangelists. Hence also it is that the Epistles of St. Peter and St. Paul [1] and St. James make no reference to the Gospels—they were not yet written. But after a time, when the Apostles and first preachers of the Gospel were either scattered abroad or were beginning to die off, and when heresies began to spring up, the want was felt of authoritative records of the life and teaching and miracles of Jesus Christ. Hence our present Gospels, in which are incorporated the earlier oral teachings, together with such other matter as each Evangelist had at his disposal.

And so it was with the writer of this Gospel. His "perfect understanding of all things from the very first" was derived partly from his acquaintance with the oral teaching above referred to, and partly from other living sources of information, such as St. Paul, possibly the Virgin Mary, probably St. Peter, St. James, and other Jerusalem Jews, whose names we do not know, and which St. Luke had not seen fit

---

[1] We shall notice two exceptions in one of St. Paul's latest epistles, by and by.

to acquaint us with. It would seem, too, from the style and contents of the two first chapters, which contain much that is peculiar to him, and is not found in any other Gospels, and much which is different in style from other parts of his own Gospel, that there existed some Aramean records of the life of John the Baptist, and of the childhood of Jesus, from which he derived his knowledge of the incidents recorded in these two chapters. Be this, however, as it may, he tells us that he had acquired a very complete knowledge " of all things from the very first"; and so it seemed good to him to set them down in order for the information of Theophilus first, and it has turned out for the benefit of the Universal Church throughout all ages.

And here I cannot help pausing for one minute to note the wisdom and the providence of Almighty God in giving to His Church these written records of all that it was important should be accurately known. While the inspired Apostles were all alive, while the oral teaching was authoritative and uniform, and the teachers and preachers were content to teach and preach only what had been "delivered" to them by the eye-witnesses, the oral teaching was sufficient. But this state of things could not last long. The Apostles, and eye-witnesses, and companions of Christ began to die off; men sprang up who were more anxious to originate doctrines of their own invention than simply to repeat what they had received; legends such as we read in the Apocryphal Gospels concerning the birth and childhood of the Virgin Mary, her marriage to Joseph, the birth and infancy of Jesus, and all manner of ridiculous miracles (Protevangelium Jacobi, Pseudo-Matthei Evangelium, the Gospel of Thomas, &c.), were in danger of being circulated among half-informed Christians; and it was inevitable that without some fixed and authoritative documents which could neither be taken away from nor added to, Christianity would be confused and corrupted, and no one could know the certainty of those things in which he had been instructed. And so God raised up the four Evangelists, and gave to His Church the four written Gospels, that as St. John says, we " might believe that Jesus is the Christ, the Son of God, and that believing we might have life through His name."

To resume. In this particular Gospel the writer seems, as I have said, to have had three sources of information. (1) The oral teaching, as we see it in those parts which occur also, word for word, in Matthew, or Mark, or both.

(2) Those living eye-witnesses, whom he had personally known, and from whose lips he had taken down the various particulars related by him. (3) Written records, which he transcribed, or otherwise used in the composition of his own narrative.

We are to enquire this evening what other evidence we have, besides that considered in our previous Lectures, for believing this Gospel to be a true and authentic history, and the genuine work of the person whose name it bears.

I do not know that I can do better than pursue the same method which we did with regard to "the Acts of the Apostles," viz. examine first the external evidence, and secondly the internal evidence of authenticity.

I. As regards the external testimony to the authenticity of St. Luke's Gospel, it may be stated, first, generally that there is absolute unanimity among all ancient writers, whether Churchmen or Heretics, as to the authorship of the third Gospel. I am well aware that, with the higher critics, unanimity of external testimony and consensus of all ecclesiastical authorities only whets the appetite of ingenious criticism to prove that they are all wrong. The Fathers of the Church, they tell us, were very credulous, they had no critical acumen, and therefore we cannot trust them. Besides, they believed in the supernatural, and that is of itself sufficient to discredit their testimony. But to those who have a little common sense, and who do not allow the Ego entirely to suppress all regard and respect for the knowledge and authority of others, it must be a matter of very considerable importance to know what they thought who lived close to the times from which we are separated by more than eighteen centuries.

Pursuing, then, the same method which we adopted in the case of " the Acts of the Apostles," I would note that Eusebius places the Gospel of St. Luke among those sacred writings —those Canonical Books of the New Testament —concerning which there had never been any doubt in the Church. Again and again he speaks of the four Gospels as undisputed. In Eusebius's time—and I would refer you to what I said about Eusebius in my first Lecture—the Gospel of St. Luke held exactly the same position in all the Churches throughout the world which it holds now. In his Ecclesiastical History, as I told you in my first Lecture, he expressly says, " Luke, by profession a physician, a constant companion of St. Paul, and intimate with the other Apostles, learnt from them the art of healing souls, of which he has left us an example in two inspired books, 'the Gospel of Luke and the Acts of the Apostles.'"

But if the Gospel held this place in the time of Eusebius you may be quite sure it did not attain it recently or suddenly. No new book could obtain such a recognition. Accordingly you would expect to find it an acknowledged book of Scripture long before the time of Eusebius. And you will not be disappointed in your expectation. We learn from that curious relic of antiquity, of which I gave you some account in my first Lecture, the Muratorian fragment, that about one hundred and fifty years before Eusebius (at latest, A.D. 170) the four Gospels headed the list of the Scriptures of the New Testament just as they do now, and that the Gospel of Luke was the third Gospel just as now. The fragment speaks of St. Luke's Gospel thus: "The third Gospel was written by Luke the physician after the Ascension of Christ," &c. (as quoted in Lecture I).

Passing over Tertullian, Origen, Clement of Alexandria, the ancient versions, &c., I pass on to Irenæus, Bishop of Lyons, about the year A.D. 180, and I quote from Dr. Davidson (p. 433), who says, "Irenæus writes, And Luke, the companion of Paul, put down in a book the

Gospel preached by him." And in another place "that Luke was inseparable from Paul, and his fellow-labourer in the Gospel, is shown by himself." And "so Luke has handed down to us those things which he had learnt from (the Apostles), as he testifies when he says, even as they delivered them unto us, who from the beginning were ministers and eye-witnesses of the Word." Again, Irenæus, as Dr. Salmon tells us (pp. 37-39), gives a variety of curious reasons why there were exactly four Gospels, neither more nor less; tells us that the four cherubims of the Apocalypse represent the four Evangelists, Luke, who "begins with the Priesthood and sacrifice of Zechariah," being the calf; and moreover quotes repeatedly (more than 100 passages) from St. Luke's Gospel.

We turn next to Justin Martyr, some thirty or forty years earlier—say A.D. 150. Dr. Davidson says "Justin Martyr was familiar with the Gospel of Luke." In fact he has at least a dozen full and clear quotations from it, and about fifty-seven altogether. It is absolutely certain that he used the third Gospel just as we do.

Again, Davidson says "Marcion (the heretic) lived before Justin. There is no doubt that he had the Gospel of Luke, which he adapted to his own ideas by arbitrary treatment." He places him A.D. 140 (see, too, Bishop Lightfoot, Essay on Supernatural Religion, p. 8, and Introduction to Gospels in Speaker's Commentary, p. 45). And lastly, coming back another fifty years, we find in Clement of Rome's First Epistle to the Corinthians, written about A.D. 95, very distinct evidences of his acquaintance with the Gospels, and with the Gospel of St. Luke in particular. In one passage, giving the general sense of a portion of the Sermon on the Mount, he uses phrases taken from both St. Matthew and St. Luke, but in which St. Luke decidedly predominates, as appears by the following quotation:—" Remembering the words of the Lord Jesus which He spake : Be ye merciful, that ye may obtain mercy ; forgive that it may be forgiven unto you ; as you do so shall it be done to you : as you give, so shall it be given unto you ; as ye judge so shall ye be judged ; as ye show kindness, so shall kindness be shown unto you ; with what measure ye mete, with the same shall it be measured to you again." *Ad Corinth.* ch. xiii. (compare Luke vi. 36–38). The passage about offences in ch. xlvi. is not so decided, and in some expressions is more like Matt. xviii. 6 than Luke xvii. 2, as, *e.g.* the word, Matt. xviii. 6 rendered in the A.V. "Cast into the sea" (καταποντίσθη) is the same as that used by St. Clement, whereas Luke has a different word (ἔρριπται).

Yet one more citation of passages in St. Luke's Gospel shall close our list. We have heard the unanimous testimony of Eusebius in the fourth century, of the many witnesses in the third, of Irenæus, Justin Martyr and Marcion, in the second; and Clement of Rome in the first. We sum up with a greater name than any of them, and of an earlier date—that of the Apostle Paul himself, who in his first Epistle to Timothy (1 Tim. v. 18) writes,—the Scripture saith—"Thou shalt not muzzle the ox that treadeth out the corn." And "The labourer is worthy of his hire." The last words were spoken by our Lord, as recorded in Luke x. 7, and are found nowhere else. And again, 1 Tim. vi. 13, "Who before Pontius Pilate witnessed a good confession," coming so soon after the preceding, may with great probability be referred to Luke xxiii. 3. The attempts to invalidate the force of all this testimony are, in my judgment, unworthy of men of truth and intelligence.

II. But does the internal evidence of the Gospel of St. Luke accord with this external testimony to its genuineness and authenticity?

Let us proceed to test the Gospel (1) by its historical accuracy; (2) by its agreement with the other Gospels; (3) by the fitness of its contents to be accepted as a true account of the Life and Teaching of our Lord and Saviour Jesus Christ. And (1) as regards the historical accuracy of the Gospel, considered as relating events which occurred at a certain epoch of the world's history, at certain places, in certain political circumstances, and in connection with certain historical personages. It is obvious that if our Gospel, professing to be written at a given time, and to relate events which occurred at a given place, and to bring into its narrative well-known persons, represented a state of things inconsistent with what is known from trustworthy secular sources of such times, places, and persons, it would be impossible for us to give credence to its contents. We should say, and say properly, this book does not speak truly or accurately of things in cases where we are able to test its accuracy and truth, and therefore we cannot trust it in matters where we are unable so to test it. It is therefore a matter of considerable moment to ascertain for ourselves whether the Gospel is accurate in its account of things earthly. And if we find, after the closest and strictest search which extensive learning can institute, that there is the most absolute and perfect agreement between the Gospel narrative and the representations of authentic history, in all matters which they have in common, then it follows that we ought to place implicit confidence in the Gospel in all matters which depend upon its single authority.

The principal persons known to history, who are mentioned in the Gospel of St. Luke, are Herod the Great, King of Judæa, Augustus Cæsar, the Roman Emperor, Quirinius, Governor of Syria, Tiberius Cæsar, the successor of Augustus, Herod Antipas, and his brother Philip, and Lysanias of Abilene, Pontius Pilate, Procurator of Judæa, and Annas and Caiaphas, the High Priests. Of these the most part are known to us from Greek and Latin historians, some from Josephus, the Jewish historian, only. And the principal events alluded to are the taxation in the time of Quirinius, the turbulent spirit of the Jews during the Procuratorship of Pontius Pilate, and the relation of the Jews and their King to the Roman Emperor.

Let us see briefly whether under each of these heads the impressions we derive from the Gospel are in accordance with those derived from the authentic history of the times.

(A) The scene is laid in the opening words

of the history (Luke i. 5) "In the days of Herod, the King of Judæa." And in ch. ii. 1–9 we learn that about a year and a half afterwards Cæsar Augustus was the Roman Emperor, and that about the same time Jesus Christ was born at Bethlehem. Here, then, you have a synchronism of three persons: Herod the Great, Augustus Cæsar, and Jesus Christ. Were these three persons alive together, as St. Luke's narrative leads us to infer they were, and as St. Matthew more distinctly affirms (Matt. ii. 1)? If they were not Luke is detected in an anachronism, and his authority is invalidated. The question is of some interest, because if the old traditional dates of B.C. and A.D. are correct, they were not alive together. Herod died B.C. 4, which would be some four years before the birth of Jesus Christ. But we now know that those old dates have no authority whatever, having been erroneously calculated by Dionysius Exiguus in the sixth century. St. Luke was quite accurate in his statement; but Herod died shortly after the birth of Christ, as St. Luke's narrative of his return to Nazareth with his parents would lead us to expect. Compare Matt. ii. 19–23. The relations of Herod the Great to Augustus, whose creature he was, are matters of history, and without any doubt.

(B) But Luke ii. 2 introduces another person into the synchronism, viz. Cyrenius (or Quirinius), Governor (or pro-Prætor, Lect. II.), of Syria, under whom the well-known taxation of Judæa took place. And his presence introduces us to one of the most difficult problems in the whole Gospel.

The only census or taxation of Judæa of which we know from secular history is that recorded by Josephus as having taken place when Cyrenius or Quirinius (which is his name in Latin, Tacit. Annal. iii. 8) was the Emperor's Governor of Syria, of which province Judæa formed a part after the death of Herod the Great. It was a very memorable event, because it gave rise to the formidable insurrection of Judas of Galilee, which is expressly referred to by Gamaliel, Acts v. 37, " After this man (Theudas) rose up Judas of Galilee, in the days of the taxing, and drew away much people after him." But this taxation took place about A.D. 6, when our Lord was about ten years old. It could not therefore be the occasion of Joseph and Mary coming up from Nazareth to Bethlehem to be taxed. Are we then to set down the statement in Luke ii. 2, as Dr. Davidson does (vol. i. 433), as one of "Luke's mistakes"? I do not think so. It appears to me that the words of St. Luke may naturally and properly be translated: *This (taxation) was the first taxation under Cyrenius Governor of Syria*[1], implying that there was a second. Now, though there is no distinct record of Cyrenius having been twice Governor of Syria, there being, as Archdeacon Farrar observes (Cambridge Bible for Schools, St. Luke, p. 62), "a singular deficiency of minute records respecting this epoch in profane historians," yet there are strong grounds for thinking that he was Governor of Syria about B.C. 4, for a short time, and then ordered the census with a view to taxation, which, however, was not fully carried out till ten years later, when he was Governor the second time. And if this is true you will observe how singularly it agrees with what we saw in considering the case of Theudas in our second Lecture. There we saw that there was a great agitation among the Jews about the taxation of their goods before what were commonly described "as the days of the taxing"; and this is exactly explained by what we here read of a "first taxa-

---

[1] "Archdeacon Farrar translates a little differently, but with the same sense substantially." This first enrolment took place (as the first) when Quirinius was Governor of Syria. "But if the article ἡ is omitted, as in the R. V., it may be construed as above. It is a further confirmation of this view that the taxation being taken according to Jewish law, by genealogy, is a certain indication that it was taken in the reign of Herod."

tion, or 'enrolment' under Cyrenius, Governor of Syria." So that this difficult passage is probably only another example of St. Luke's exact historical knowledge of the times which he is writing about. I would add that the words of Justin Martyr, "When the first taxation under Cyrenius was taking place in Judæa" (Dialog. cum Tryph. Jud., p. 303), seem fully to bear out this view.

(c) The next personage we have to do with is Tiberius Cæsar, and those associated with him in Luke iii. 1. St. Luke evidently wishes to mark as distinctly as he can the precise year when the ministry of John the Baptist began. So he mentions the fifteenth year of the reign of Tiberius Cæsar (dating from his being associated in the Empire by Augustus); and for greater certainty, mentions also the Tetrarchs, or rulers of the various provinces which made up the old kingdom of Judæa, or had been afterwards reckoned as belonging to Judæa, who simultaneously governed their respective dominions. You will also remember that the circumstances related in chapters i. and ii. of the birth of John the Baptist and of Jesus, and the age of Jesus recorded in iii. 23 as that at which He began His ministry, necessitate the occurrence of the above synchronism at something less than thirty years from the death of Herod. St. Luke therefore has spared no pains to fix an exact point in chronology, and it is a signal proof of his accuracy that he cannot be convicted of a single error. His assignment of the right name to each of the tetrarchs of these several petty countries speaks also to the carefulness of his research[1], as well as his knowledge of the divisions of the ancient kingdom of Judæa. It should be added that St. Luke's account of Herod Antipas's incestuous marriage with his niece (the wife of another Philip different from the Tetrarch mentioned in iii. 1), and his allusion to the murder of John the Baptist (ix. 9), are fully confirmed by Josephus (Antiq. xviii. 5).

(D) Pontius Pilate comes next under our notice. In him we have a notorious person spoken of by Tacitus, Josephus, and Philo. Tacitus mentions that Christ "suffered a malefactor's death under Pontius Pilate the Procurator." All the accounts we have of him show that under his government the Jews, provoked by his tyranny and his frequent insults to their religion, were unusually turbulent.

---

[1] Lysanias, Tetrarch of Abilene, is the only one who cannot be identified with absolute certainty. The name was hereditary in the family, like that of Herod.

Josephus mentions that on two occasions two or three thousand Jews had been massacred at the Passover by the Roman soldiers, and the Temple courts filled with dead bodies. Something of the kind is probably what St. Luke alludes to (ch. xiii. 1), when he speaks of the blood of certain Galileans having been mingled by Pilate with their sacrifices. Anyhow, the incident entirely accords with Pilate's character and the events of his Procuratorship. In like manner the mention of the insurrection of Barabbas exactly fits the time when it is said to have happened; it was evidently one of the frequent insurrections which Pilate's tyranny was continually provoking. And then as regards the conduct of Pilate himself at our Lord's trial before him. Pilate was for some reason most unwilling to condemn Jesus. At least three times (xxiii. 4, 14, 20, 22) he declared His innocence of any crime, and professed his desire to release Him. Whether it was that he scorned and hated the superstition of the Jews, which he saw was at the bottom of their desire that Jesus should be crucified, or that he was impressed with the innocence of Jesus, and awed by the majesty of His demeanour, or that he was influenced by fears and scruples on account of his wife's dream recorded by St. Matthew (Matt. xxvii. 19), one thing is clear, he was strongly bent on releasing Him. His remitting the case to the jurisdiction of Herod, the Tetrarch of Galilee, as soon as he heard that Jesus had to do with Galilee (xxiii. 5-7) and his offer to release Him, according to the Passover custom of granting an amnesty to one criminal at the choice of the people, are further evidences of this strong desire. Why then did he not set at nought the wishes of the people whom he despised and hated, as he had so often done before, and acting upon his own convictions, let Jesus go free? The state of affairs at Rome, or rather at Capreæ, where Tiberius was, exactly explains it. The gloomy tyrant Tiberius, whose portrait is so strongly drawn by Tacitus, and by Juvenal, was at this period of his life more than ever suspicious and revengeful. The recent treason and death of his former favourite Sejanus, by whose interest Pilate had been appointed Procurator some years before, had stimulated his suspicion, and made him more savage than ever. Pilate had been already once reprimanded by Tiberius for disturbing his Province by outraging the superstitions of the people[1]; and in point of fact, he was ultimately deprived of his government by the Emperor Caius Caligula in consequence of an

[1] Philo ad Caium.

accusation of violence laid against him by the Samaritans. It was a known point of policy with Tiberius that the provinces should be kept tranquil. If, then, in the present state of Tiberius' mind, with Pilate's connection with Sejanus acting as a provocation rather than as a protection, the ungovernable fury of the Jews should lead to an embassy to Tiberius to complain of Pilate's acts of violence, cruelty, and oppression, and if, above all, this complaint was accompanied with the accusation that whereas the Jewish nation in their loyalty to Cæsar had demanded the execution of a seditious man who claimed to be himself the King of the Jews, and went about stirring up the people, and forbidding them to pay tribute to Cæsar, Pontius Pilate had refused to have justice done, and had set the prisoner free, it is manifest that not only Pilate's government, but his very life, would have been in danger. Accusations of high treason (læsæ majestatis) were not things to be risked in the days of Tiberius any more than in the days of Henry VIII. Hence Pilate's decision to content a people whom he hated, by putting to death the man whom he wished above all things to save.

We may also note in this connection the accuracy with which the complicated relations between the petty tetrarchs, or kings, and the supreme Roman government, are exhibited. Pontius Pilate, the Emperor's Procurator of Judæa, exercises sovereign power at Jerusalem, where he resides, probably in the palace of Herod. Herod Antipas is there for a time only, and as a stranger, to keep the Passover. But when it appeared that Jesus was a Galilean, and so a subject of Herod Antipas, the tetrarch of Galilee, Pilate handed him over ($ἀνέπεμψεν$, the legal technical term) to Herod's jurisdiction. It has been conjectured, too, with much probability that the quarrel between Pilate and Herod, mentioned in xxiii. 12, had been caused by some invasion of Herod's rights, or contempt of his authority, by Pilate, perhaps in the very matter of the cruel insult to the Galileans alluded to in Luke xiii. 1, and that Pilate adroitly seized this opportunity of wiping out the former insult by a studied deference to Herod's authority in the matter of this Galilean prisoner. Be this however as it may, we see in the narrative how thoroughly conversant the writer of St. Luke's Gospel was with the political circumstances of the different parts of Palestine in the times of which he is writing. Had the scene been laid in the reign of Herod the Great, who was an allied king (Rex Socius) of the whole country, or of Archelaus, whose government included

Judæa, the representation of the trial would have been wholly out of harmony with the truth. It may also be observed that St. Luke never calls Herod Antipas king, as St. Matthew and St. Mark do (Matt. xiv. 9; Mark vi. 22, 25, 26, and 29), but only by his legal title of tetrarch. With equal accuracy he gives the title of *king* to Herod Agrippa in Acts xii. 1, 20. "There was no portion of time for thirty years before, nor *ever* afterwards, in which there was a *king* at Jerusalem . . . except the last three years of this Herod's life" (Paley's Evidenc., p. 209). Josephus tells us that Caligula put the crown upon his head, and that Claudius added Judæa to his dominions (Antiq. xviii. and xix.).

(E) One word as to the persons named in iii. 2, Annas and Caiaphas, and the title of High Priest given to them both. Caiaphas was at this time the High Priest acknowledged by the Romans, having been appointed between three and four years before. Annas had been High Priest for seven years, but was deposed by the arbitrary power of the Roman Procurator, Valerius Gratus, some fifteen years before; and there had been three High Priests between him and his son-in-law, Caiaphas. But Annas, from his wealth and influence, and from the fact that in the eyes of strict Jews he had not been legally deposed, continued to occupy a commanding position among the priests, and doubtless was considered at least as the Sagan, or deputy High Priest. It is in accordance with this that we read in John xviii. 13, that they took Jesus bound "to Annas first"; and that, in v. 19 of the same chapter, Annas is apparently called "the High Priest," as he is also distinctly in Acts iv. 6. It may be added that Caiaphas was deposed about a year after our Lord's crucifixion.

(F) But, besides the accuracy of the writer in his account of historical events and persons, we see indications of a contemporary well-informed historian in a variety of allusions and minor incidents. Thus (a) Luke xx. 22, we have the incident of the tribute money (compare Luke xxiii. 2). The question of the lawfulness of a Jew paying tribute to the heathen government was one fiercely agitated at the time, and dividing the opinions of Pharisees and Herodians. (b) In Luke xix. 12 sqq., our Lord's parable about a nobleman going to a far country to receive for himself a kingdom and to return, draws its significance from actual facts in recent Jewish history. Both Archelaus and Herod Antipas, as Josephus relates (A. J. xvii. 9), went to Rome to receive from Augustus the kingdom left to them by their father's will; and Archelaus, after a reign of ten years, was so hated by his subjects for his cruelty that "they would not have him to reign over them" any longer, but procured his banishment to Gaul, after which Judæa was governed by a Roman Procurator (A. J. xvii. 11). (*c*) The title on the cross, written in three languages, Greek, Latin, and Hebrew (Luke xxiii. 38 ; John xix. 20) is another notable example. Why was it written in three languages ? Plainly that all who stood around might be able to read and understand it. But how came it about that to secure this end a trilingual inscription was necessary ? Because in point of fact at that particular time there were three distinct populations living in Palestine, and three distinct languages in common use. There were the Jews, who spoke a Hebrew, or Aramean dialect, as their native speech. There were the Greeks, who from the time of Alexander the Great and his successors, the Seleucidæ, and the Ptolemies, were the cultivated and upper commercial class ; there were the Romans, who as conquerors, formed the official and military classes.

That our Lord sometimes, if not always, as some think, spoke Hebrew or Aramean, we have several examples : as when He said to the deaf and dumb man, whose ears He opened, " Ephphatha," that is " Be opened " (Mark vii. 34) ; to Jairus's daughter, "Talitha cumi," which is, being interpreted, " Damsel, I say unto thee arise " (Mark v. 41); to Simon, " Thou shalt be called Cephas," which is by interpretation, a stone (in Greek, Peter), John i. 42 ; when He surnamed the sons of Zebedee " Boanerges, which is, The sons of Thunder " (Mark iii. 17) ; when He cried on the cross " Eloi, eloi, lama sabacthani?" which is, being interpreted, " My God, My God, why hast Thou forsaken Me ? " (Mark xv. 34). Other instances of the use of Aramean are the surname of the Apostle Simon, the Kananite (not Canaanite as A.V.) Matt. x. 4 ; Mark iii. 18, of which the Greek translation is given (Luke vi. 15; Acts i. 13) Zelotes, the zealot; the place Golgotha, which is, being interpreted, " the place of a skull " (in Latin, Calvary), Mark xv. 22 ; John xx. 17 ; a place called " The Pavement," but in the Hebrew, " Gabbatha " (John xx. 13); the field called in their proper tongue, " Acel dama," that is to say, " the field of blood " (Acts i. 19). I may add " Rabbi," which is to say, being interpreted, " Master " (John i. 38) ; "the Messias," which is, being interpreted, "the Christ " (A. V. 41); " Tabitha," which is, by interpretation, " Dorcas " (Acts ix. 36); and " Elymas " the " sorcerer," for so is his name by interpretation (Acts xiii. 8).

You will all remember, too, how St. Paul addressed the Jewish multitude from the stairs at Jerusalem, in the Hebrew tongue (Acts xxi. 40; xxii. 2), and what a marked effect it had upon his hearers. But the same Paul, when he addressed the chief Captain, Claudius Lysias, spake to him in Greek. And all St. Paul's Epistles were written in Greek. It was a very ancient belief in the Church that St. Matthew's Gospel was originally written in Hebrew or Aramaic; but the other Gospels were written in Greek.

Then with regard to Latin, we see the influence of the Latin tongue on the Greek spoken at this time in the Province of Judæa in the number of Latin words clothed in Greek form. The words for "scourged" (Matt. xxvii. 26); "the common hall" (*ib.* 27); "the watch" (xxviii. 11); "the napkin" (John xi. 44; xx. 7); "tribute" (Matt. xxii. 17); "Centurion" (Mark xv. 39); "a penny" (Matt. xx. 2); "a farthing" (Matt. v. 26), and many others are all Latin words. The same prevalence of Latin-speaking people made Latin one of the three languages that were current in Palestine at this time, especially in the army, and among people who had to do with the soldiers. Thus the trilingual inscription on the cross is a significant mark of contemporary and authentic history.

The agreement of the Gospel of St. Luke with the other Gospels need not detain us long. That the general view given by this Evangelist of the person and miracles, the life and doctrine, the death and resurrection, of Jesus Christ our Lord, is the same as that given by the other synoptic Evangelists, is, I believe, disputed by nobody, and is patent to the most unlearned observer. St. Luke differs from the other Gospels chiefly in the introduction of new matter. For example, the two first chapters have no parallel in the other Gospels. The details of the birth of John the Baptist, the several canticles, the abode of Joseph and Mary at Nazareth before the Nativity, the circumcision of Christ, His presentation in the Temple, the visit to Jerusalem and disputing with the Doctors in the Temple when He was only twelve years old, are all peculiar to St. Luke. The entire section, Luke ix. 51 to xviii. 14, is nearly, if not entirely, independent of the other synoptists, especially of St. Mark, with whom in the verses immediately preceding Luke had been in the closest accord. Luke alone mentions the bloody sweat, the healing of the ear of the High Priest's servant, &c. So again in the account of the trial before Pilate, Luke alone mentions the episode of our Lord being sent to Herod; he alone mentions the conversion of the penitent thief; the journey to Emmaus; our Lord's exposition of the prophecies concerning Himself in the law of Moses, in the Prophets, and in the Psalms; and the particulars of the Ascension. On the other hand, he omits many things which are recorded by St. Matthew or St. Mark, or by both of them; as for example, the visit of the Magi from the East, and the flight into Egypt; the beheading of John the Baptist; our Lord's walking on the sea; the feeding of the four thousand; the opening the eyes of the blind man at Bethsaida, and many others. It is also true that in some cases, as in the report of our Lord's "Sermon on the Mount," in Matt. v.-vii., and in Luke vi. 20-49, it is difficult, if not impossible, to decide whether the close resemblances indicate that we are reading the account of the same discourse at the same time and place, or whether the wide differences indicate that we have to do with different discourses spoken at different times and in different places. But all this is consistent with perfect accuracy on the part of the different writers, who were guided by different motives in what they related and what they omitted; who may not each have had the same knowledge which the others had, though they related

truthfully what they did know; and who by
their consensus in all main points of their
common narrative give us a feeling of absolute
certainty in regard to those things wherein we
have been instructed. The harmony of the
synoptists generally, and of St. Luke in particular, with St. John, is of another kind, because
St. John wrote his Gospel for a special purpose
and from a special stand-point; described mainly
the Judæan and not the Galilean ministry, and,
for the most part, trod the same ground as the
synoptists only at the commencement and at the
close of the Gospel history. Still the general
agreement is absolute and complete; and St.
John may be said to add an important testimony
to the authenticity of the Gospel of St. Luke, by
the concurrence of his witness to Christ with
that of the third Gospel.

We turn to take a brief survey of the contents
of the Gospel to see whether or no it gives us a
worthy view of our Saviour's life and teaching,
or whether, like the apocryphal Gospels, it
betrays a merely human origin by its unworthy
representation of the character and actions of
the Son of God. And I think that no one who
combines a sound intellect with a spiritual mind
can make himself acquainted with the Jesus of
the Gospel of St. Luke without being penetrated

by the conviction that he has been conversing with a Divine Person, and that the pen which drew that portraiture is worthy of its subject. Whether we see Him confronting the Great Adversary of man in the Wilderness of the Temptation, or preaching the Gospel of deliverance to the poor, the broken-hearted, and the captives, in the synagogue of Nazareth; whether we see Him turning the sorrow of death into the joy of life at the gate of Nain, by brief words of pity and power, or hear Him pouring out those inimitable accents of rebuke to the Pharisee, and of mercy and grace to the penitent and much-loving sinner at His feet; or whether we see Him with calm majesty rebuking the winds and the waves, or bidding the Ruler's daughter awake from the sleep of death and return to her weeping parents;—surely we feel that we have before us the very Christ, the Son of God, the Friend of man. Can He, too, be less than Divine who uttered "The Parable of the Sower," who preached "The Sermon on the Mount," who rebuked spiritual pride, and put hope and strength into the hearts of penitent sinners by the Parables of "The Prodigal Son," and of "The Pharisee and the Publican in the Temple?" And the tears shed over Jerusalem, the city which was about to crucify Him; and the lowly triumph as He rode into her streets upon the ass's colt amidst the joyous "Hosannahs" of His disciples; and the agony in the garden; and the good confession before Pontius Pilate; and the intercession for His murderers as He hung upon the cross; and His words of power and of love to the thief dying by His side; and the rising from the dead; and the deep teachings on the way to Emmaus; and the hands, still marked with the glorious shame of the crucifixion, uplifted to bless His Church as He was parted from her, and rode on the clouds to His throne in heaven; I say do not these things, told with the inimitable simplicity of the beloved Physician, do they not bear the stamp of truth, and reveal to us a Saviour who indeed came down from heaven to save us? Indeed, so strong is the inward witness which the Gospel bears to its own truth and Divine origin that, when once it has lit its sacred fire in a believer's heart, and the Saviour whom it reveals is known and loved there, there is no longer any need of the outward evidences of authenticity: Jesus Christ is seen and known in the light of His own glory, and in the virtue of His own transforming and sanctifying power.

And now I think we may close this part of our enquiry with a full sense of satisfaction.

We noticed at the outset that there was an evidence of the authenticity of St. Luke's Gospel which no other Gospel had, viz. that borne to it by "the Acts of the Apostles." But then it became necessary to test the value of that evidence by ascertaining the authenticity of the Book which bore it. Accordingly we proceeded to examine carefully the external and internal evidences of the authenticity of "the Acts," which, with the evidences of identity of authorship in the two works, occupied us fully to the end of our third Lecture. And to my mind those evidences were so thorough and complete that I should have been quite content to accept the first verse of "the Acts of the Apostles" as a sufficient and decisive proof of the authenticity of St. Luke's Gospel. I thought it well, however, to see what further evidence of the authenticity of this Gospel could be supplied, *first* from the unanimous external testimony of early Christian writers, and *secondly* from the internal evidence of the Gospel itself, tested by its historical accuracy, and by its harmony with the other Gospels, and by the moral fitness of its portraiture of the Lord Jesus Christ. This we have done to-night: and it now only remains for us to consider the place which the Gospel of St. Luke holds in the general evidences of the truth of the Christian Religion. This will be the subject of our concluding Lecture.

LIST OF BOOKS CHIEFLY USED IN THE FOREGOING LECTURE.

Westcott's Canon of the New Testament.
Salmon's Introduction to the Study of the New Testament.
Dr. Davidson's Introduction to the New Testament.
Professor Norton's Genuineness of the Gospels.
Introduction and Commentary on St. Luke in Speaker's Commentary.
Archdeacon Farrar on St. Luke in Cambridge Bible for Schools.
Roberts's Discussion on the Gospels.
Josephus's Jewish Antiquities.

LECTURE V.

On entering upon this last phase of our enquiry we leave behind us all uncertainty as to the authorship and date of the Gospel we have been considering, and shall base our argument henceforth upon its being the work of Luke, the companion and friend of St. Paul, as upon a demonstrated and acknowledged fact. And, we have to consider what bearing this Gospel has upon the question whether or no Christianity is true, and how far it challenges our acceptance of it as truth, as the necessary act of a rational mind, and the solemn duty of a reasonable moral agent.

I. I would ask you in the first place to consider upon what, in the common affairs of life, our belief of things, of which we are not cognizant by our own senses of seeing and hearing, habitually rests. I see you all before me, and you see and hear me. Neither you nor I therefore need any external evidence of my lecturing to this audience to-night in this place, nor as to the subject-matter of the Lecture which is being delivered to you. We stand in the place of eye and ear witnesses. But those who are not present, but who may wish to know something of our proceedings this evening, will read the report in the newspaper, or will ask questions of their friends who are present, and so will arrive at some knowledge of what has been said and done in this room. Their knowledge will rest entirely upon evidence, evidence oral and written. And if it should happen a hundred years hence that any curiosity should exist about our "society for promoting higher religious education" at the close of this nineteenth century, and about the lectures delivered in connection with it, the evidence supplied by the contemporary issues of the Bath newspapers, and still more any original copies which might survive of the Lectures themselves, would be of great value in satisfying such curiosity, and establishing the truth concerning the society. Or, to apply the same idea to a wider field, why do you believe that Julius Cæsar came to Britain nearly two thousand years ago? Well, you believe it because it is a matter of notoriety that he did; you know that other people of learning and adequate information believe it, and that nobody doubts it. But if you look more closely into the subject you find that there is an undoubted work written by Julius Cæsar himself, in which he gives an account of his invasion of Britain; that the authenticity of these commentaries of his is attested by writers either contemporary or living soon after[1], and that the fact of his having been in Britain is attested or alluded to by many trustworthy historians. Your belief in Julius Cæsar's expedition to Britain rests entirely upon evidence, but it amounts to absolute certainty.

And it is the same with almost all the incidents and actions of our every-day life. We depend upon the testimony of others. Some things we know by the evidences of our own senses, but, for our knowledge of most of the things by which our daily actions are guided, we depend upon the oral or written testimony of other men.

But some one will say, what a lot of falsehoods men have believed upon the testimony of others. What heaps of false beliefs, superstitious tales, mere myths, incredible wonders, absurd adventures, impudent impostures, transparent lies, have obtained credence in the world upon the evidence of men who were either deceived themselves, or intentionally deceived others. This is perfectly

---

[1] By Cicero, Suetonius, &c.

true, and the warning given to us by such misplaced credulity is one we shall do well to attend to, viz., in matters of importance to be very careful to sift the evidence, and see whether it is trustworthy or not. Are the witnesses men of good character for truth and honesty? Had they ample opportunities of judging whether the things they have reported really happened, and happened in the way and at the time in which they said they did? And were they competent judges of the truth of the things which they report? If they fail in any of these particulars then we are at liberty to doubt or absolutely to reject their evidence. But if they are unimpeachable in all these respects then we are *not* at liberty either to doubt or to reject. Sufficient evidence not only invites, but claims as its right, our implicit belief. To reject adequate testimony to truth, because some people have believed falsehood upon inadequate testimony, is like rejecting wholesome food because some people have taken poison by mistake.

II. Let us then in the next place examine St. Luke's credentials, and carefully consider his claims as a witness to the truth of the Christian faith. (1) As to his personal character and qualifications: They are given to us by St. Paul in two words, the "*Beloved Physician*"

(Col. iv. 14). One indicates his moral qualities, the other his intellectual qualifications. Luke had been Paul's intimate friend and companion for at least ten years (Acts xvi. 10, xxviii. 30). He had shared his labours in preaching the Gospel of Christ in Asia and in Europe (Acts xvi. 10). He had shared the fatigue of his constant journeys by land and by sea. He had braved with him perils among the heathen, and perils among fierce and bigoted Jews. He had taken counsel with him when the first bold stride was made from Asia into Europe (Acts xvi. 10). He was with him in the house of Lydia; and, doubtless, was among those who were "comforted" when Paul and Silas came forth from the dungeon at Philippi (Acts xvi. 40). In Paul's last journey from Philippi to Jerusalem, at those touching prayer-meetings at Miletus and at Tyre, through those days of hourly peril at Jerusalem, during the long confinement at Cæsarea, in the eventful voyage to Melita, and the march to Rome (Acts xxviii. 11-16), and the two years' imprisonment there (Acts xxviii. 30), Luke was ever with him (Col. iv. 14). And the result of this long and chequered intercourse, the result of those various situations in which the man's qualities—his faith, his courage, his steadfastness, his sincerity, his piety, his affection, his resources, his wisdom, his good judgment—would be put to the test, and tried to the uttermost, the result, I say, was that when St. Paul speaks of him in one of the letters written from his prison in Rome, he speaks of him as the "beloved Physician." I think this is a good testimonial as to character. If St. Paul loved him after ten years of closest intimacy, amidst events of the most searching character, I think I can trust him not wilfully to deceive me. I may add that we have another pleasant evidence of Luke's faithfulness. in that three or four years later, when St. Paul was again in prison at Rome, just before his martyrdom, St. Luke was still by his side. Demas had forsaken him, others were at work in different places, but the beloved Physician would not leave him in the hour of extreme danger. "Only Luke is with me" (2 Tim. iv. 11) is the last mention by the Apostle of his beloved friend. But (2) the words of St. Paul are a guarantee for his intellectual qualifications as witness for Christ. The profession of a physician is one which pre-eminently requires learning, knowledge, sagacity, and judgment. The habits of close observation, nice discrimination, accurate diagnosis, and careful statement, are the essential features of a physician. We usually find, too, that the close and intimate knowledge of individual men, which the physician's calling naturally entails, produces a knowledge of human character, and an acquaintance with human motives, beyond that of ordinary men. The physician sees men in their unguarded moments, in the privacy of their homes, at times when confidential communications are necessary. He is led, too, to receive with caution statements made to him by his patients, and carefully to test the symptoms of disease, for fear of being led into error, and so to a wrong treatment of the case. He knows the difference between the τεκμήρια[1] the "infallible proofs," and symptoms of disease (Acts i. 3), and the mere σημεῖα, *i.e.*, symptoms which are not infallible. He is skilled in making a diagnosis of the difficult cases brought before him. And this professional habit naturally induces a similar habit of caution in matters which are not professional.[2] We have then, in Luke's calling as a physician, a guarantee that we have not to deal with a credulous, thoughtless, careless retailer of mere gossip, and ignorant tales, but with a sensible and discriminating observer, used to test things reported as facts,

[1] See Lecture III.
[2] Compare the passage in Ecclesiasticus, ch. xxxviii.

and to make a difference between random assertions and trustworthy evidence of competent witnesses.

And this estimate of Luke's qualifications, which the mere statement of his being a physician would lead us to form, is fully borne out by the two works of his which have been handed down to us. In both of these we see the man of education, we see the refined thoughts and the polished language which betray culture, and bear witness to intellectual power. I think it is Renan who says of the Gospel of St. Luke—*C'est le plus beau livre qu'il y ait*—"It's the most beautiful book in the world." And nobody can read either it, or the book of the Acts of the Apostles, without being charmed with the beautiful simplicity of the style, and the graphic power of the descriptions, as well as with the elevation of the sentiments which he delights to express, coupled with the modesty of entire self-suppression. As far, then, as personal character and intellectual qualifications go, we have in St. Luke a most unexceptionable witness.

But (3) something more than personal high character, and mental qualifications, is required to make a competent witness of the works and teaching of such an one as Jesus Christ during the three-and-a-half years of His ministrations on the earth. He must have had opportunities of acquiring exact and perfect knowledge of what he purposes to relate, or else with the best intentions he may lead his readers astray. Had St. Luke such opportunities?

Place yourselves in imagination at about the year A.D. 53, when we are first brought into contact with St. Luke. Who was then the centre of all the life and energy and power by which the faith of the Lord Jesus Christ was being borne with irresistible force through the heathen nations of the world, turning the world upside down, to use the expressive phrase of the Thessalonian rioters, and gathering both Jews and Gentiles into the Church of God? Who but the great apostle of the Gentiles, St. Paul? He had seen Jesus Christ (1 Cor. ix. 1), he had received from the Lord Himself the Gospel which he preached, how that Christ died for our sins according to the Scriptures, and that He was buried, and rose again the third day according to the Scriptures, that He was seen of all the Apostles, and last of all of Paul himself. To him, too, was given an abundance of revelations; he had been caught up into the third heavens, and heard unspeakable words (2 Cor. xii. 2–4). His were all the gifts of the Holy Spirit in extraordinary abundance (1 Cor. xiv. 18). No one so conversant as he with all the mysteries of the Kingdom of God. And Luke was his intimate friend and companion for at least ten years. Can you imagine a better school for learning all about the Christian faith than such a companionship as that? And think of the rest of the society in which Luke lived. There were Timothy and Titus, and Silas and Judas, and Mark, and Barnabas, and Aristarchus, and Gaius, and Tychicus, and Trophimus the Ephesian—all those who under the great leadership of Paul had built up the kingdom of God in Asia and Europe. In the society of such men, so earnest, so devoted, so well instructed in the faith, and with such an inquiring and acquisitive mind, and such a devout spirit, as Luke's was, we can readily conceive what perfect knowledge he would acquire of everything relating to the person and work and doctrine of Jesus Christ our Lord.

But these were not his only sources of information. For "many days" he tarried in the house of Philip, the Deacon and Evangelist, at Cæsarea (Acts xxi. 8-10), and from him might have learnt some particulars about the closing scenes of our Lord's life on earth. On his arrival at Jerusalem he was introduced to James, the

Bishop, and to all the Elders of the Church at Jerusalem (Acts xxi. 18). During the two years of St. Paul's confinement at Cæsarea he would have frequent opportunities of converse with James and the Elders, and others who had known Jesus Christ in the days of His flesh. While there, too, he might have visited Gethsemane, and wandered over the Mount of Olives, and walked out to Bethany, and from the descent of the mountain have looked down upon Jerusalem, as Jesus did, and he may have stood on Calvary, he may have seen Joseph's new tomb in which the body of Jesus had lain; and this *admonitus locorum*—these local memorials—would give that vivid colouring to his narrative which is so charming to the reader. All these opportunities he certainly had within his reach.

But I think it is probable that he had other opportunities to which we have no direct clue. We know nothing of St. Luke's early life. The tradition—an early one recorded by Eusebius—that he was born at Antioch may, or may not, be true. He may have been at Jerusalem long before that visit which is recorded in Acts xxi., and may have known St. Paul many years before he joined him at Troas, as we gather that he did from Acts xvi. 10. But we have no direct information on the subject. It does seem likely, however (though not certain), from St. Luke's language (Luke i. 2-3) that he had become acquainted with Christianity in very early days, and had received its truths from the lips of Apostles themselves, as Eusebius says he did. It is also a probable inference from the particularity of his account, in "the Acts," of St. Peter's sayings and doings, and of his long discourse on the day of Pentecost, and, in the Gospel of St. Peter's denial, and of his entering into the sepulchre, and one or two other particulars, that St. Luke was acquainted with Peter, and had received some information from him.

And then, besides these opportunities of personal converse with the Apostles and other eyewitnesses of the Word, he had the advantage of seeing written records of various kinds which have long since perished. In my last Lecture I pointed out that the two first chapters of the Gospel were almost certainly derived from some written Aramean source. St. Luke tells us also himself of the many who, before him, had taken in hand to set forth a declaration of those things which were most surely believed among Christians. This clearly does not point to apocryphal Gospels, full of myths, such as sprung up later, and of which some, such as the Protevangelium of James, the Gospel of St. Thomas, the history of Joseph the carpenter, the acts of Pilate and others, are extant at the present day. The age of myth, and apocryphal imitations of the Canonical Gospels, had not come yet. The writings of which St. Luke speaks "set forth in order a declaration of those things which were most surely believed by Christians." They would contain authentic accounts of miracles, of parables, of teachings, of particular events, probably of the birth, and death, and resurrection, of Jesus. Though true as far as they went, they might be quite insufficient, or they might contain many unintentional errors, amidst much valuable truth. And so, though quite unfit to be "the Gospels" of the Church, they might supply much valuable material to one who, like St. Luke, was able to reject the false, and retain only the true.

Then there would be, probably reduced to writing, either in Aramean, or in Greek, or in both, the stereotyped oral teaching of the Apostles from which the catechetical teaching of the Church's Pastors, and Evangelists, and Prophets was drawn, and of which we find the traces in those passages of verbal identity which are found in the synoptic Gospels.

But besides these, writing as he did before the fall of Jerusalem, and that wholesale destruction of archives which took place there, Luke would have access to divers public records, both Jewish and Roman. One such we have at length in the third chapter of St. Luke's Gospel; I mean the genealogy of Jesus Christ through Joseph, his reputed father. It is manifest that as the taxation, or enrolment, ordered by Augustus Cæsar, was carried out in Judæa according to Jewish ideas (no doubt by King Herod the Great's arrangement)[1], and that every man was enrolled in the city to which by his genealogy he belonged, not in that to which he belonged by the accident of residence, there must have been in each the exhibition of the genealogy in virtue of which each citizen claimed to be enrolled in such or such a city. Just as we read in the days of Ezra, that those who returned from the Babylonish captivity came up all in due genealogical order, and that some who could not find their register—they claimed to be priests—were put aside till the matter could be decided by a priest with Urim and Thummim (Ezra ii. 3-63). Evidently then St. Luke found still existing the pedigree in virtue of which Joseph went to Bethlehem to be enrolled—with

---

[1] This is a strong incidental evidence that the "first taxation" took place in the reign of Herod the Great; see Lecture IV.

Mary, his espoused wife—because Bethlehem was the city of David, and he was of the house and lineage of David.

There must, also, have been extant in the Roman archives some record of the trial before Pontius Pilate, from which St. Luke may have derived some of the particulars which are not mentioned in the other Gospels. But this is only conjectural.

(4) There is one other condition of considerable importance which tends to add greatly to our confidence in the truth of any narrative, viz., that it should have been published in the lifetime of those who were conversant with the persons and the events which form the subject of the narrative. Now we have seen (Lecture III.) that the Gospel of St. Luke must have been published before A.D. 63, because Luke, writing "the Acts" in that year, speaks of the Gospel as "the former treatise." And it seems to me highly probable that he wrote it at Cæsarea during St. Paul's two years imprisonment there. That would be about A.D. 59 or 60; say some twenty-six or twenty-seven years after the crucifixion. Now there must then have been a large number of Christian people still alive, and still in middle age, amongst whom the memory of our Lord's presence on earth was still fresh and living.

To circulate a book, professing to give an accurate history of His life, which was not in harmony with their recollections, would have been an absurdity. Such a book would have taken no hold upon the mind of the disciples, but would have been rejected with contempt. So that we have a strong additional confirmation of the truth of St. Luke's Gospel, in the fact that it was published in the lifetime of numbers of men and women who were our Lord's contemporaries, and had personal knowledge of His human life on earth.

We may sum up then this part of our argument by saying that every qualification, but one, which is calculated to command our implicit confidence in the truth of any history—high moral and intellectual excellence in the writer, exceptional opportunities of ascertaining the exact truth, and the acceptance of his authority as unimpeachable by his contemporaries and their successors through eighteen centuries—all meet in the third Gospel. The one qualification that is wanting is that of an eye-witness, which he himself tells us he did not possess. But the other qualifications are so full and complete, and what Luke tells us is so entirely in accordance with what we learn from others who were eye-witnesses, that this want in no way detracts from his thorough credibility as the historian of the life and doctrine of the Divine Author of the Christian Faith.

III. Having then established upon solid grounds St. Luke's thorough trustworthiness, and his claims to be believed in what he tells us in his Gospel, we must enquire in the last place what it is that he tells us, that we may know whether his Gospel comprehends all the articles of the Christian faith.

(1) He teaches us very plainly the cardinal doctrine of the Christian faith, the INCARNATION of our Lord Jesus Christ. There are very many who are willing to accept Jesus Christ as their teacher and leader, who admire His holy life, His beneficent actions, and His constancy even unto death. They admit the lofty morality of His doctrine, the unrivalled beauty of His Parables, perhaps even the truth of His prophecies, and, on the strength of this, they call themselves Christians. But they do not believe in the Divine nature of Jesus Christ as the Son of God. They do not believe that the Word, which was in the beginning, and which was with God, and was God, was made Flesh, and dwelt among us. But this cardinal truth of the faith St. Luke distinctly teaches; for, after recording the angel's message to the Blessed

K

Virgin, "Thou shalt conceive in thy womb, and bring forth a Son, and shalt call His name Jesus; He shall be great, and shall be called the Son of the Highest .. and He shall reign for ever, and of His kingdom there shall be no end," he adds the angelic explanation, "The Holy Ghost shall come upon thee, and the power of the Highest shall overshadow thee, therefore, also, that Holy Thing which shall be born of thee shall be called the Son of God." And so, throughout the Gospel, Luke records the voice from Heaven at our Lord's Baptism, "Thou art My Beloved Son" (iii. 22). He records the confession of the Tempter conveyed in the words, "If Thou be the Son of God cast Thyself down from hence" (iv. 9); that of the unclean spirits at Capernaum, "Thou art the Holy One of God—Thou art Christ, the Son of God" (iv. 34, 41); that in the country of the Gadarenes, "What have I to do with Thee, Jesus, thou Son of God most High" (viii. 28). He records the voice which came out of the cloud at the Transfiguration, saying, "This is My Beloved Son, hear ye Him" (xx. 2). He repeats Peter's confession, "Thou art the Christ of God" (ix. 20); and the Lord's prophecy of His coming "in His own glory" (ix. 26). He is careful to preserve our Lord's own testimony to His mysterious nature: "No man knoweth who the Son is but the Father, and who the Father is but the Son, and he to whom the Son shall reveal Him" (x. 22); and His assertion of a far higher dignity than that of David's Son, viz., that of David's Lord (xx. 14). In his pages we read the memorable confession made before the Chief Priests and Elders, when they asked Him, "Art Thou the Son of God?" "Ye say that I am" (Luke xxii. 70, xxiii. 3). And through the whole Gospel the same Divine character is maintained. The words, the actions, the promises, the claims, the powers put forth, are not those of a Moses, a Samuel, or an Elijah, but they are those of God's Christ, the only Begotten and Eternal Son of the Eternal Father.

(2) St. Luke teaches those essential doctrines of the Christian faith, the Death and Resurrection from the dead of Jesus Christ, the Son of God. After faithfully recording the Lord's prophetic announcement to the Disciples that "the Son of Man must suffer many things, and be rejected of the Elders and Chief Priests and Scribes, and be slain, and be raised the third day" (ix. 22); and telling us how, "when the time was come that He should be received up, He steadfastly set His face to go to Jerusalem"

(ix. 51); thus indicating not only His foreknowledge of the death which He was about to die, but His own fixed purpose to offer Himself as a sacrifice for the sins of the world, Luke goes on to relate with a marked tension of spirit the successive steps of our Lord's life which were leading towards that stupendous end. Again and again he notes that the Lord was going to Jerusalem (xiii. 22, 34; xvii. 11; xviii. 31; xix. 11); and the significance of this is shown by the words of Jesus, "Behold, we go to Jerusalem, and all things that are written by the Prophets concerning the Son of Man shall be accomplished; for He shall be delivered unto the Gentiles, and shall be mocked, and spitefully entreated, and spitted on, and they shall scourge Him, and put Him to death" (xviii. 31–33). In the discourses and actions of our Lord, recorded by St. Luke at this time, we seem to feel the influence of the approaching crucifixion. It filled the Lord's thoughts, it tinges the whole of St. Luke's narrative. And then came the end. With what inimitable pathos, with what sublime simplicity, with what an awful sense of their solemn significance, does Luke lay before us the details of the closing scenes of the life of Jesus! The Passover Supper, the agony in the Garden, the successive trials before the High Priest, and Herod, and Pontius Pilate, the mocking and scourging, the majesty of the patient Sufferer, His undying pity for Jerusalem, His prayer for His murderers, His pardon of the dying thief, the darkened sun, the rending of the veil of the Temple, the giving up of His spirit into His Father's hands: all this, enhanced by the wailings and lamentations of the women that followed Him, by the confession of the dying malefactor, and the noble testimony of the Centurion, shows what a place in St. Luke's conception the death of the Lord Jesus held, and what a place he desires it should hold in the minds of his readers.

And in like manner in his account of the Resurrection. We not only see the historian's desire to present such a statement of details before his readers as should remove all occasion or possibility of doubt, but we see, also, the consciousness of the Evangelist of the momentous import to the salvation of the world of the dogma he was propounding, that Christ, who was crucified, dead, and buried, did indeed rise again from the dead, according to the Scriptures, and did ascend into Heaven, there to sit at God's right hand until His coming again in glory.

(3) And if we add to all this the fulness of

our Saviour's teaching, as recorded by St. Luke, in His Parables and discourses, in His exhibitions of the Divine grace and mercy, *e. g.*, in the Parables on "The Prodigal Son," "The Publican and the Pharisee," "Dives and Lazarus," in the "Call of Zaccheus," and in many other passages; His exhortations to prayer; His warnings of the coming judgment; His withering denunciations of hypocrisy and mere outside religion; His frequent testimony to the work of the Holy Ghost (i. 15, 35, 41, 67; ii. 26; iii. 16, 22; iv. 1, 14, 18; xi. 13; xii. 12); and the abundant appeals to the authority of the Scriptures of the Old Testament (i. 70-73; ii. 22; iii. 4-6; iv. 4, 8, 12, 17-21; vii. 27; ix. 30, 31; x. 26; xi. 31, 32, 49; xiii. 28; xvi. 16, 31; xvii. 14; xviii. 20; xx. 27, 42; xxiv. 27, 44), we see at once that the Gospel of St. Luke comprehends the whole Christian faith, and that to believe it as an authentic record of the life of the Lord Jesus, is to believe in Christianity itself. If the Gospel is authentic and true, Christianity is true likewise.

Here then our subject properly ends. If I have proved by many "infallible proofs," by external and internal evidence, that this Gospel was written by Luke the Physician, the beloved friend and companion of St. Paul, before the year A. D. 63 (and probably about A. D. 60), and that its authenticity carries with it the truth of the Christian religion, then I have a right to claim the full acceptance of the Christian faith by all before whom this evidence is laid, as the necessary act of a rational mind, and as the solemn duty of a reasonable moral agent. And our subject is come to an end.

But there is one point intimately connected with our subject on which I wish to say a few words before we part, both to avoid the danger of misapprehension of what I have said, on your part, and because it seems to me important to the due understanding of the evidence of Holy Scripture. I mean the INSPIRATION of the sacred historians.

You have, perhaps, noticed that in considering the authenticity of the Gospel of St. Luke, and the sources of his information, and the special opportunities enjoyed by him of acquiring a thorough knowledge of the facts and truths of Christianity, and the consequent claims he has upon our confidence, I spoke throughout as I should speak of any secular author, and without any reference to the inspiration of the writer. A moment's reflection will, I think, make it clear why I did so.

As a matter of fact, the Gospels and Epistles,

in which the events and doctrines of the Gospel are exhibited to us, come before us as so many documents claiming our attention because they are true. And their truth, like that of any other documents, is subject to investigation and critical examination. The sacred writers themselves refer us to their earthly qualifications as witnesses of Christ's truth. Our Evangelist, Luke, demands our confidence on the score of his having had perfect understanding from the very first of all things which are most surely believed among Christians, and having received the knowledge of them from those who from the beginning were eye-witnesses and ministers of the word, In "the Acts of the Apostles" (Acts i. 3), he dwells upon the fact that the Resurrection of Jesus Christ was made certain to His Apostles by many infallible proofs, He being seen of them, and having conversed with them, not once or twice, but through a period of forty days. St. Peter, in his address in the house of Cornelius (Acts x. 41), lays stress upon the fact that Jesus not only openly showed Himself alive to His Apostles, but did eat and drink with them after He rose from the dead. St. Paul in writing to the Corinthians (1 Cor. xv. 5–8), to refute the deadly error of some among them, who said that there is no resurrection of the dead, appeals to the evidence of Peter and the eleven Apostles, and of the five hundred brethren who had seen Him at once, and to that of James, and to his own experience, to establish the truth of the resurrection of Christ. St. Peter, in laying down the necessary qualifications of an Apostle to be chosen in the room of the traitor Judas, says that he must be one who had companied with the other Disciples all the time that the Lord Jesus went in and out among them, from the Baptism of John till the Ascension of Christ (Acts i. 21, 22). You will all remember how our Lord appealed to the senses of the Apostles as to the certainty of His resurrection, "Behold, My hands and My feet, that it is I Myself: handle Me and see, for a spirit hath not flesh and bones as ye see Me have" (Luke xxiv. 39). And to Thomas " Reach hither thy finger, and behold My hands, and reach hither thy hand and thrust it into My side ; and be not faithless but believing" (John xx. 27). St. John, too, at the close of his Gospel, appeals to the truth of his own testimony for the credibility of his Gospel (John xx. 31 ; xxi. 24), and, in exactly the same spirit, writes in his first Epistle, " That which we have heard, which we have seen with our eyes, which we have looked upon, and our hands have handled ... declare we unto you" (1 John i. 1–3). In all these instances the sacred historians themselves do not say to us "I am inspired by the Holy Ghost, and therefore everything I say is infallibly true, and must be believed without enquiry or hesitation." But they give us the means of knowing that they could not be mistaken or deceived, and that their testimony may, with all confidence be received. In considering, therefore, the credibility of St. Luke's Gospel, the question of his inspiration did not properly arise. We had to think and speak of him merely as an historian, and to show what a right he had, merely as such to our implicit confidence.

But it would be a grave error to infer from this that St. Luke did not write under the inspiration of the Holy Spirit. The truth is that that wonderful accuracy which marks his writings; that right judgment which enabled him to reject everything which was false or useless, and to retain only such things as would be profitable to the Church; and that perfect knowledge of our Lord's words which he has communicated to us with such simplicity and power, are the results of that inspiration. It was one of the offices of the Holy Spirit, as promised by our Lord (John xiv. 26), to bring to the remembrance of the Apostles whatever Jesus had said to them. And, in like manner, it was not by superseding, but by strengthening and enlarging the other natural powers of their minds, that the Holy Ghost enabled the sacred writers to be such faithful recorders of what they had heard and seen, or had received directly from those who from the first had been ministers and eye-witnesses of the word. And doubtless it is an immense additional comfort to a Christian when reading in the Gospels the record of the teaching and works of Jesus Christ, to know that he is reading the words not only of honest and capable men, but of men specially selected and qualified by God's Holy Spirit to be the teachers of the Church throughout all ages.

And now I have only to thank you for the attentive hearing which you have given me; and to express the hope that however imperfectly I have handled the important matters we have been considering, yet some things may have been said which will give you a clearer and fuller notion of the impregnable grounds on which our Faith rests than perhaps you had before. It is my own firm belief that the evidences of the truth of the Christian Faith never have been, and never can be, refuted; but that the judgment of the intellect, the affections of the heart, and the assurance of faith, all agree in the conclusion that the Christ of the Gospels is the Saviour of the world. If by God's blessing I have assisted any one of my hearers to arrive at the same conclusion, or, in this unbelieving generation, to hold it with a firmer grasp, to the unspeakable comfort of his soul, I humbly thank Almighty God, and take courage.

LIST OF BOOKS CHIEFLY USED IN THE FOREGOING LECTURE.

Eusebius' Ecclesiastical History.
Evangelia Apocrypha (Apocryphal Gospels), Tischendorf.
Genealogies of our Lord Jesus Christ, by Lord Arthur Hervey.
Dictionary of the Bible, Article "Gospels," by the Archbishop of York.

PUBLICATIONS

OF THE

SOCIETY FOR PROMOTING CHRISTIAN KNOWLEDGE.

HISTORY OF INDIA.

From the Earliest Times to the Present Day. By Captain L. J. TROTTER. With eight full-page Woodcuts on toned paper, and numerous smaller Woodcuts. Post 8vo. Cloth boards, 10s. 6d.

SCENES IN THE EAST.

Consisting of twelve Coloured Photographic Views of Places mentioned in the Bible, beautifully executed, with Descriptive Letterpress. By the Rev. CANON TRISTRAM, Author of "Bible Places," "The Land of Israel," &c. 4to. Cloth, bevelled boards, gilt edges, 6s.

SINAI AND JERUSALEM; OR, SCENES FROM BIBLE LANDS.

Consisting of Coloured Photographic Views of Places mentioned in the Bible, including a Panoramic View of Jerusalem with Descriptive Letterpress. By the Rev. F. W. HOLLAND, M.A., Demy 4to. Cloth, bevelled boards, gilt edges, 6s.

BIBLE PLACES; OR, THE TOPOGRAPHY OF THE HOLY LAND.

A succinct account of all the Places, Rivers, and Mountains of the Land of Israel mentioned in the Bible, so far as they have been identified; together with their modern names and historical references. By the Rev. CANON TRISTRAM. With Map. Crown 8vo. Cloth boards, 4s.

THE LAND OF ISRAEL.

A Journal of Travel in Palestine, undertaken with special reference to its Physical Character. By the Rev. CANON TRISTRAM. Fourth edition, revised. With Maps and numerous Illustrations. Large post 8vo. Cloth boards, 10s. 6d.

NARRATIVE OF A MODERN PILGRIMAGE THROUGH PALESTINE ON HORSEBACK, AND WITH TENTS.

By the Rev. ALFRED CHARLES SMITH, M.A., Rector of Yatesbury, Wilts, Author of "The Attractions of the Nile," &c. Numerous Illustrations and four Coloured Plates. Crown 8vo. Cloth boards, 5s.

THE NATURAL HISTORY OF THE BIBLE.

By the Rev. CANON TRISTRAM, Author of "Bible Places," &c. With numerous Woodcuts. Crown 8vo. Cloth boards, 7s. 6d.

A HISTORY OF THE JEWISH NATION.

From the Earliest Times to the Present Day. By the late E. H. PALMER, M.A., Author of "The Desert of the Exodus," &c. With Map of Palestine and numerous Illustrations. Crown 8vo. Cloth boards, 4s.

THE ART TEACHING OF THE PRIMITIVE CHURCH.

With an Index of Subjects, Historical and Emblematic. By the Rev. R. ST. JOHN TYRWHITT. Cloth boards, 5s.

AUSTRALIA'S HEROES.

Being a slight Sketch of the most prominent amongst the band of gallant men who devoted their lives and energies to the cause of Science, and the development of the Fifth Continent. By C. H. EDEN, Esq., Author of "Fortunes of the Fletchers," &c. With Map. Crown 8vo. Cloth boards, 5s.

SOME HEROES OF TRAVEL;
OR,
CHAPTERS FROM THE HISTORY OF GEOGRAPHICAL DISCOVERY AND ENTERPRISE.

Compiled and re-written by W. H. DAVENPORT ADAMS, Author of "Great English Churchmen," &c. With Map. Crown 8vo. Cloth boards, 5s.

CHRISTIANS UNDER THE CRESCENT IN ASIA.

By the Rev. EDWARD L. CUTTS, B.A., Author of "Turning Points of Church History," &c. With numerous Illustrations. Post 8vo. Cloth boards, 5s.

HEROES OF THE ARCTIC AND THEIR ADVENTURES.

By FREDERICK WHYMPER, Esq., Author of "Travels in Alaska." With Map, Eight full-page and numerous small Woodcuts. Crown 8vo. Cloth boards, 3s. 6d.

CHINA.

By Professor ROBERT K. DOUGLAS, of the British Museum. With Map, and eight full-page Illustrations on toned paper, and several Vignettes. Post 8vo. Cloth boards, 5s.

RUSSIA: PAST AND PRESENT.

Adapted from the German of Lankenau and Oelnitz. By Mrs. CHESTER. With Map, and three full-page Woodcuts and Vignettes. Post 8vo. Cloth boards, 5s.

Depositories:
LONDON: NORTHUMBERLAND AVENUE, W.C.
43, QUEEN VICTORIA STREET, E.C.
BRIGHTON: 135, NORTH STREET.

www.ingramcontent.com/pod-product-compliance
Lightning Source LLC
Chambersburg PA
CBHW030304170426
43202CB00009B/868